DISCARDED

150 Best of the Best House Ideas

150 Best of the Best House Ideas

Francesc Zamora Mola

HARPER
DESIGN
An Imprint of HarperCollins Publishers

HarperCollins books may be purchased for educational, business, or sales promotional use.
For information, please email the Special Markets Department at SPsales@harpercollins.com.

First published in 2016 by:
Harper Design
An Imprint of HarperCollins*Publishers*
195 Broadway
New York, NY 10007
Tel.: (212) 207-7000
Fax: (855) 746-6023
harperdesign@harpercollins.com
www.hc.com

Distributed throughout the world by:
HarperCollins*Publishers*
195 Broadway
New York, NY 10007

Editorial coordinator: Claudia Martínez Alonso
Art director: Mireia Casanovas Soley
Editor and texts: Francesc Zamora Mola
Layout: David Andreu Bach

ISBN 978-0-06-244463-9

Library of Congress Control Number: 2015960140

Printed in China
First printing, 2016

CONTENTS

INTRODUCTION

Establishing a place to live is the prime basis of residential architecture. House design is complex, and many subjects are decided during the design process.

While some of us are looking for the challenge of a clean slate, others prefer to concentrate on remodeling an existing house. Regardless of which one we choose, houses accommodate many basic functions, and are designed to conform to our needs and to our lifestyle; but they also go beyond that, expressing an attitude toward life.

The design of homes is intrinsic to the expression, at a general level, of the changing values and lifestyles, and at a personal level, of our self, our tastes, and our interests, to the point that, for many of us, our homes are part of who we are. The process of designing a house is a story told through the emplacement—or site—which creates a sense of place and establishes relationships with its surroundings; through building technology, which speaks of form and function; and through the materials it's built with, expressing a vocabulary of aesthetic, economic, and environmental significance. The sense of place describes the quality of our relationship with physical settings, meanings, and activities. It is critical to establish a sense of place not just to anchor a building to a specific location, but also to create an environment sensible to our human nature. In this respect, the selection of the site may affect the comfort of the house built on it, and consequently, our well-being.

Environmental factors including climate—defined by solar exposure, wind patterns, and precipitation—and site characteristics—such as size, shape, topography, landscape features, and site accessibility—can provide clues for approaching the development of a site and deciding how much outdoor spaces will be used.

The way the site is used affects the form of the house, which is a series of parts assembled in a functional, economic, and cultural way. As lifestyles evolve and values change, the configurations of houses explore new languages that have to do with massing, rhythms, balance, openings and breaks in the walls, light and shadow, and indoor-outdoor connections. The home is no longer defined by the enclosure, but through a new concept of space, which often translates into the extension of the living spaces to forge a form of living indoor and outdoor. The selection of materials reinforces the architecture's formal language, giving it character and presence, but it never is frivolous and rarely based only on aesthetic criteria.

The design process—from the selection of the site to the determination of materials—involves discussions with architects, engineers, designers, neighbors, community design review groups, and city officials. Codes and regulations, which determine the minimum construction standards, beginning with land use, building height, fenestration, energy efficiency, and safety, are aimed at reconciling design with appropriateness in relation to the context, whether urban, suburban, or rural.

Choosing a site, whether urban, suburban, or rural, is as much a lifestyle choice as designing a house. Homes may only occupy a parcel of land, but to many of us, they mean a whole world.

From the merely functional and comfortable dwellings to the luxury abodes, from houses that reflect outdoor lifestyles in rural areas to homes conveniently located in urban communities, houses are designed to be respectful of their environment, while infusing modern sensibility for aesthetics, functionality, ecology, and technology.

A large lot, conveniently located near a shopping and restaurant area and close to a park in a sought-after neighborhood of Washington, DC, presented a desirable opportunity for a young family to build a new house. Designed to respect both the scale of neighboring houses and the rhythm of the streetscape, the new building aligns with adjacent houses, while retaining the vast majority of mature trees and green space located between the street and the house. The house appears relatively solid when viewed from the street with strategically placed windows ensuring privacy to the street-facing spaces.

Brandywine House

Robert M. Gurney, Architect

Washington, District of Columbia, United States

© Anice Hoachlander, Allen Russ

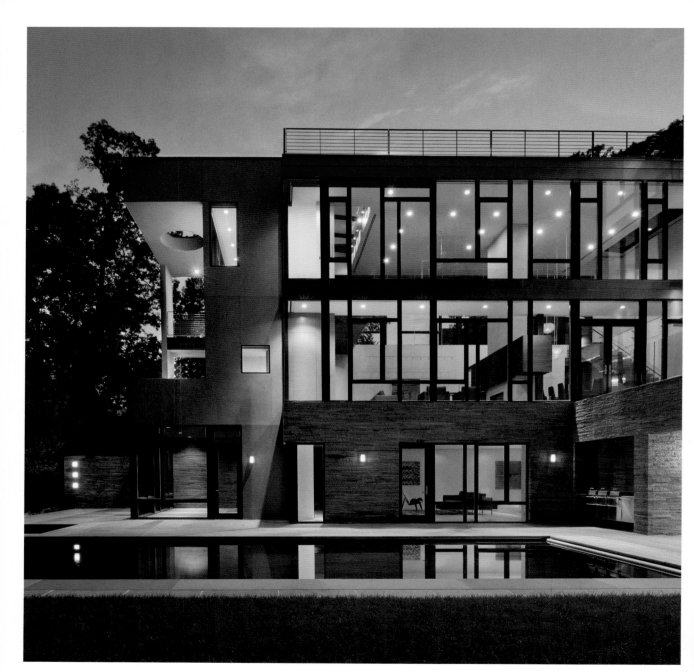

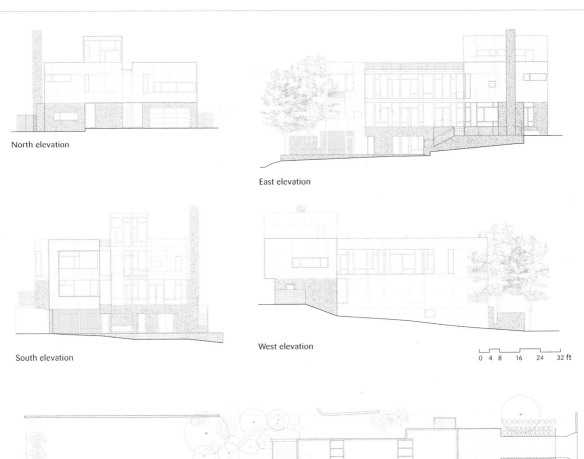

North elevation

East elevation

South elevation

West elevation

0 4 8   16   24   32 ft

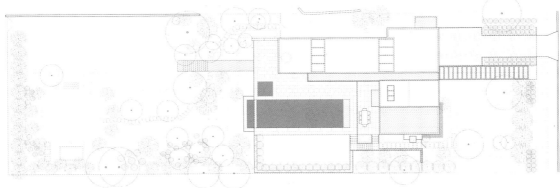

Site plan

0 5 10   20   30   40 ft   ⊖ N

Third floor plan

Fourth floor plan

Ground floor plan

Second floor plan

0 4 8   16   24   32 ft   N

The L-shaped house is organized around
the outdoor living spaces and swimming
pool, and is oriented toward the large,
south-facing rear yard, and the wooded,
less manicured landscape beyond.

001

The placement of a pool on a site is generally determined by its relationship with other structures, orientation, and sun exposure, before its size and proportions are defined.

Floor-to-ceiling expanses of glass
provide ample visual and physical
connectivity to the terraces, the
swimming pool, and the wooded
landscape beyond.

The interiors are warm, light-filled, and ordered with a clear spatial organization. Various wood species, including white oak, Santos mahogany, rosewood, and various zebrawoods —all forest certified or reconstituted products—combine with limestone and various granites to provide a rich material palette.

002

Allow various wood tones
to coexist in a single space.
Just as if you were choosing
a paint color scheme, select
a dominant wood finish, and
one or two more to create
accents.

Despite the relatively large size of this house and the extensive use of glass, the house remains incredibly energy efficient. While the large number of windows and skylights provide generous day lighting, computer-programmed shading devices modulate solar gain.

003

The orientation of a bedroom influences the positioning and the size of windows. Sightlines and sun path need to be taken into consideration in order to optimize comfort.

004

Long bands of clerestory windows create the effect of floating roofs. The light entering a room through a clerestory window is diffuse, minimizing shadows and dark areas.

Set on a verdant plot, this house is nestled between three large trees. It is conceived as an assembly of two rectangular blocks connected by a third narrow, transparent block containing the staircase. This assembly creates the framework for a central courtyard, where an existing flowering tree, set beside a reflective pool, becomes the visual centerpiece for the entire house. The desire to visually connect to the tree and to the central courtyard resulted in a highly transparent threshold between the built and the open spaces.

Three Trees House

DADA & Partners

New Delhi, India
© Ranjan Sharma of Lightzone India

The central courtyard with its reflective pool, infinity pool, and stone pavement engages with the transparent and folding built edge of the house.

The shaded north-facing courtyard is
further animated with different rooms
fronting onto it along with the deep
overhangs providing a continuous
play of light and shade.

005

The tradition of using an existing natural feature as an organizing element has transcended cultural boundaries and has stood the passage of time.

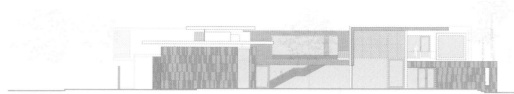

North elevation

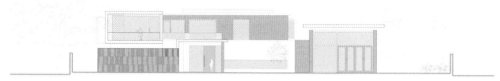

East elevation

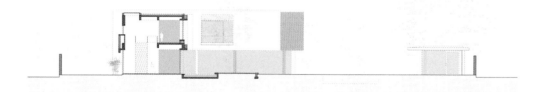

Section through the staircase block and central courtyard

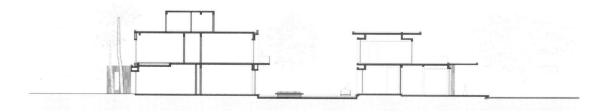

Section through the east and west block

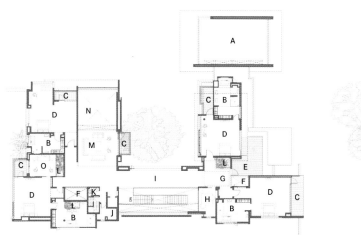

Second floor plan

A. Drawing room
B. Bathroom
C. Balcony
D. Bedroom
E. Terrace
F. Light well
G. Lobby
H. Puja room
I. Corridor
J. Pantry
K. Powder room
L. Light shaft
M. Upper lounge
N. Double height space
O. Study

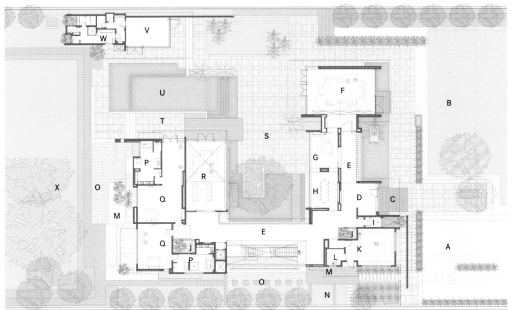

Ground floor plan

A. Drop-off area
B. Front lawn
C. Entry porch
D. Entry lobby
E. Corridor
F. Drawing room
G. Bar
H. Dining room
I. Powder room
J. Light well
K. Kitchen
L. Utility
M. Deck
N. Kitchen garden
O. Gravel court
P. Bathroom
Q. Bedroom
R. Living room
S. Courtyard
T. Pool deck
U. Pool
V. Fitness studio
W. Steam and sauna
X. Rear lawn

N

006

When surrounded by rooms or circulation on all sides, a courtyard becomes an inwardly focused feature. Light and air reaching this central element can affect the rooms around it.

007

Skylights mainly provide light to an interior space, where windows are not a possible option. However, they can also be used to complement a space with windows to balance out the light, while adding architectural character.

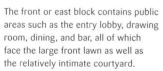

The front or east block contains public areas such as the entry lobby, drawing room, dining, and bar, all of which face the large front lawn as well as the relatively intimate courtyard.

The spatial experience of a room is enhanced by the physical qualities that define it, such as proportions, light, color, texture, and its connecting elements with adjacent spaces—for instance, doors, windows, stairs, and courtyards.

008

A master bedroom with a private outdoor space is the ultimate relaxing retreat; a room away from all gathering spaces and in touch with nature.

009

The bathroom is, beyond question, the room of the house that can easily transport your body and mind to a state of serenity and well-being. Sunlight, water and vegetation are ideal for creating a one-of-a-kind experience.

A house of two halves, the two-story "Quad"-inspired front portion takes advantage of park views from the first-floor master bedroom and living room. A single-story pavilion-like structure accommodates the kitchen, meals, and living area at the rear. A double-sided fireplace separates the meals and living space, where exposed concrete blocks mimic the external piers. Generous outdoor living includes a large loggia and kitchen overlooking the rear garden and the pool.

Alphington House

InForm

Melbourne, Victoria, Australia
© Derek Swalwell

010

Protected exterior areas make
an easy transition between
the interior and the exterior.
They can be easily equipped
with a kitchen or a fireplace,
turning this sheltered spot
into the ultimate extension
of a living area.

011

Most window and door manufacturers offer endless customized designs that adapt to any wall design, both technically and aesthetically.

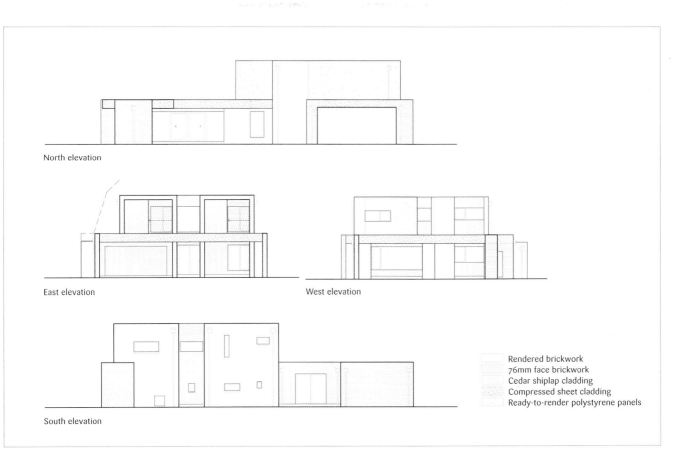

North elevation

East elevation

West elevation

Rendered brickwork
76mm face brickwork
Cedar shiplap cladding
Compressed sheet cladding
Ready-to-render polystyrene panels

South elevation

012

The massing of a building, its proportions, and the relation between walls and openings can contribute to the minimization of energy loads and optimization of natural energy.

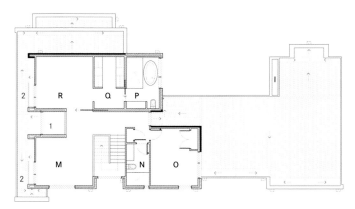

Second floor plan

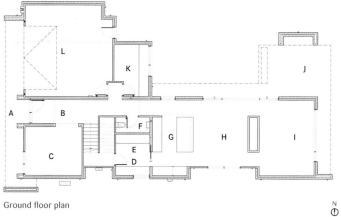

Ground floor plan

1. Void
2. Screen

A. Porch	J. Loggia
B. Entry	K. Office
C. Study/guestroom	L. Garage
D. Pantry	M. Family room
E. Laundry	N. Bathroom
F. Powder room	O. Bedroom
G. Kitchen	P. Master bathroom
H. Dining room	Q. Walk-in-closet
I. Living room	R. Master bedroom

N

013

A central feature wall can be a focal point around which a space is organized, separating different functions while maintaining an open feel.

014

A renewed interest in freestanding tubs has led manufacturers to create lines of plumbing fixtures inspired by the same concept.

This small house is designed for outdoor living, open to the sky, and sensitive to its site and to its neighbors. Though small in footprint, generous glass and volume create luminous inside-outside spaces. The largest room is the yard, with a trellis-shaded dining area, and a swimming pool with a wood deck. A more intimate courtyard is just outside the living room.

Volumetric subtractions create unexpected formal effects. The house presents a narrow façade to the street, leaving a wide gap with its neighbor that allows diagonal views of the side of the house.

Field House

John Friedman Alice Kimm Architects

Santa Monica, California, United States

© Benny Chan/Fotoworks

Field House

015

Screens in front of windows
are an architectural detail
that adds visual interest to
a building's façade, while
providing shade and minimizing
solar gain.

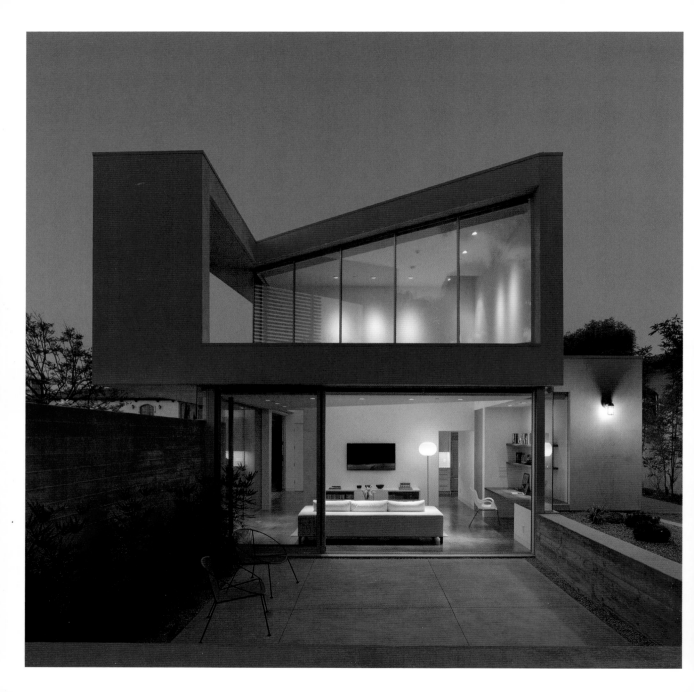

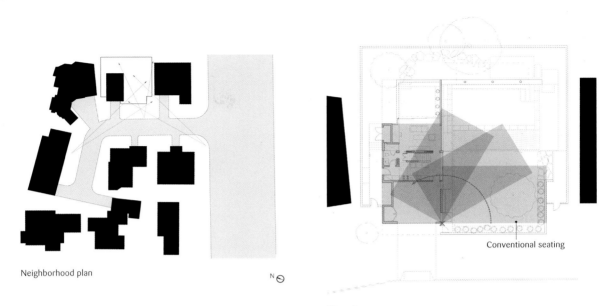

Neighborhood plan

Conventional seating

Hinge diagram

N

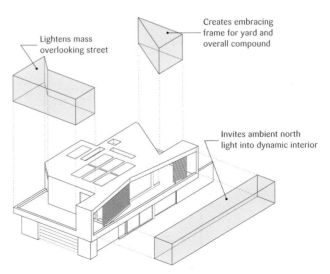

Lightens mass overlooking street

Creates embracing frame for yard and overall compound

Invites ambient north light into dynamic interior

Exploded axonometric diagram. Sculptural identity

Second floor plan

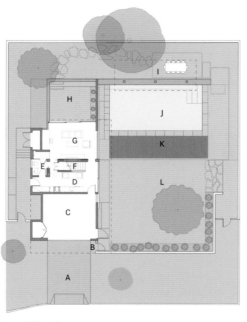

Ground floor plan

A. Grasscrete driveway
B. Main entrance
C. Garage
D. Kitchen/Indoor dining
E. Bathroom
F. Staircase
G. Living area/guestroom
H. Private garden
I. Outdoor dining
J. Pool
K. Wood deck
L. Lawn
M. Gravel roof
N. Open to below
O. Wood screen
P. Bedroom

0 4 8   16 ft   N ⊖

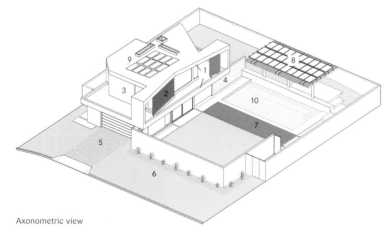

Axonometric view

PASSIVE DESIGN
Minimized footprint conserves resources and maximizes ground permeability. Narrow floor plan promotes natural ventilation and maximum daylight penetration.

1. South-facing eaves block summer light, but allow in winter light.
2. FSC-certified wood screen limits heat gain and provides privacy for bedroom.
3. Minimized west-facing openings keep out punishing afternoon sun.
4. Concrete wall creates heat sink for living room.

MATERIALS – PART 1/2
5. Grasscrete driveway promotes water absorption.
6. 90% drought-tolerant plants and subsurface irrigation conserve water.
7. FSC-certified decking.

ACTIVE DESIGN – PART 1/2
8. Photovoltaic panels on "solar trellis" produce 3.9 kW of power.
9. Solar water heating pads pre-heat water and conserve energy.
10. Automatic pool cover conserves water and heat.

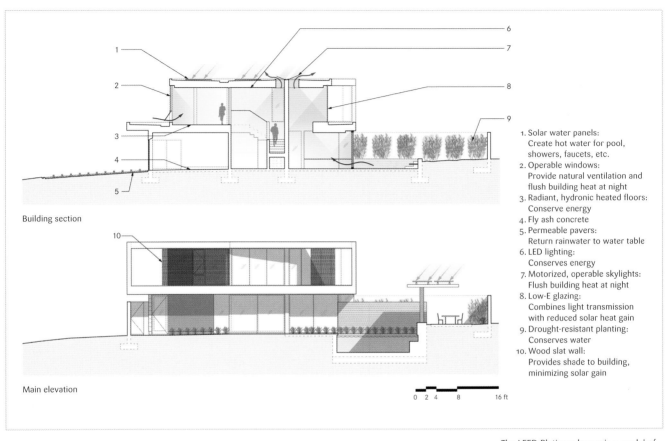

Building section

Main elevation

1. Solar water panels:
   Create hot water for pool,
   showers, faucets, etc.
2. Operable windows:
   Provide natural ventilation and
   flush building heat at night
3. Radiant, hydronic heated floors:
   Conserve energy
4. Fly ash concrete
5. Permeable pavers:
   Return rainwater to water table
6. LED lighting:
   Conserves energy
7. Motorized, operable skylights:
   Flush building heat at night
8. Low-E glazing:
   Combines light transmission
   with reduced solar heat gain
9. Drought-resistant planting:
   Conserves water
10. Wood slat wall:
    Provides shade to building,
    minimizing solar gain

0 2 4   8   16 ft

The LEED Platinum house is a model of
integrated sustainability, in which its
green strategies—including solar water
panels, radiant hydronic heated floors,
permeable pavers, Low-E glazing, and
LED lighting—are seamlessly integrated
into a unique sculptural aesthetic.

The structure's thick frame embraces
the yard, while shading the house's
southern façade. The triangular
cutout above the office gives the
room a dramatic spatial appeal, while
introducing generous amounts of
ambient northern light.

016

Not only will a skylight brighten up a space, but it will also add character to it. If placed near a wall, it will allow sunlight to wash down the surface and reflect into the room.

017

UV rays are responsible for
fading fabrics, drying wood,
and deteriorating artwork.
Window coverings or window
tints can minimize damage on
your interiors.

018

Natural stone gives a
bathroom a spa-like touch,
while the continuous run of
tiles creates an open feel.

This single-family house serves multiple generations with a dynamic, light-filled design that provides flexibility by providing common spaces where the members of the family gather, but yet they can still enjoy the privacy of their designated areas in the house. Despite a generational zoning, the interior spaces flow smoothly to stress the unity of the family. Another aspect of this project is the importance of natural light and how it enters the house as part of a design strategy aimed at implementing sustainable solutions.

Holleb Residence

John Friedman Alice Kimm Architects

Santa Monica, California, United States

© Benny Chan/Fotoworks

019

Terraces are a valuable outdoor space regardless of the size. They are a coveted commodity—especially in densely populated areas—that home buyers are willing to pay extra for.

The structure's sustainability is expressed through skylights or natural day lighting, screens for shading, solar thermal panels to heat the pool, and photovoltaic panels.

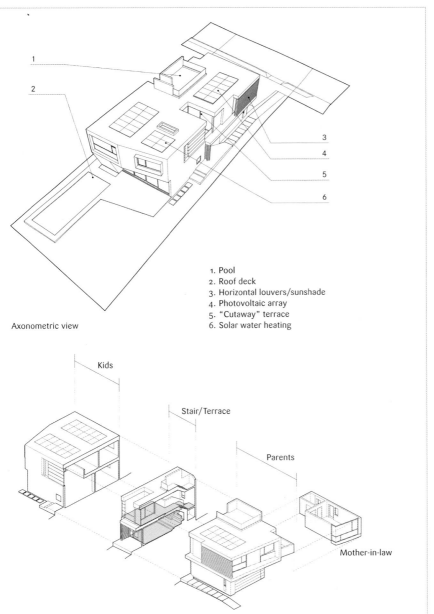

1
2

Axonometric view

1. Pool
2. Roof deck
3. Horizontal louvers/sunshade
4. Photovoltaic array
5. "Cutaway" terrace
6. Solar water heating

3
4
5
6

Kids

Stair/Terrace

Parents

Mother-in-law

Exploded axonometric view

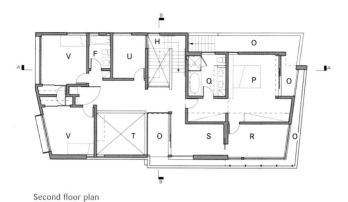

Second floor plan

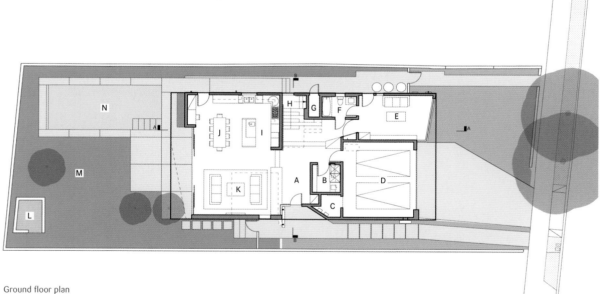

Ground floor plan

A. Entry
B. Laundry room
C. Mechanical room
D. Garage
E. Flexible space/
   guestroom
F. Bathroom
G. Storage

H. Staircase
I. Kitchen
J. Dining area
K. Living area
L. Roof deck
M. Garden
N. Pool
O. Terrace

P. Master bedroom
Q. Master bathroom
R. Office
S. Sitting area
T. Open to below
U. Studio
V. Bedroom

0 2 4 8   16 ft   N

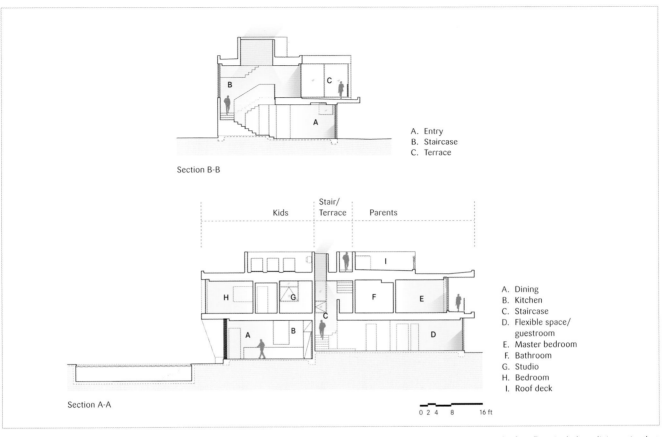

Section B-B

A. Entry
B. Staircase
C. Terrace

Kids | Stair/Terrace | Parents

A. Dining
B. Kitchen
C. Staircase
D. Flexible space/
   guestroom
E. Master bedroom
F. Bathroom
G. Studio
H. Bedroom
I. Roof deck

Section A-A

0 2 4 8   16 ft

The first floor includes a living suite that can be separately accessed. Above, a master suite is separated from the kids' domain by an eight-foot slot containing the stair and a "light notch" activating the double-height living room.

020

Clerestory windows enhance the architectural appeal of a double-height space, filling a room with uniform lighting.

The sculptural kitchen light monitors above the island echo the faceted geometry of the house's back façade, creating interplay between surfaces and light.

021

The sculptural aesthetic of a staircase can serve to enhance the spatial experience of an interior space, through its location, shape and materials.

A narrow terrace aligns with the staircase to split the second floor: the master suite to the south and the kids' rooms to the north. Delimited by glass on three sides, the terrace funnels natural light down to the double-height living room.

022

In urban environments, bedrooms oriented toward a backyard are more protected. They are also, to some degree, less exposed to views from neighboring houses, which allows for a design of rooms with large windows.

Located at the bend of a meandering river, Rock River House provides panoramic views of glistening water below and the forested nature preserve beyond. The program is organized on a narrow wedge of land creating a series of indoor and outdoor spaces, which recall a nearby crescent-shaped waterfall edge. The main levels of the home are woven together by a ribbon of mahogany starting at the sunlit conservatory and ascending to an upper studio.

Rock River House

Bruns Architecture

Rockton, Illinois, United States
© Tricia Shay Photography

The façade is clad in reclaimed redwood
from a decommissioned local building,
remilled and selectively wire-brushed
to craft a larger composition. Stone
harvested from a neighboring Wisconsin
quarry completes the exterior palette.

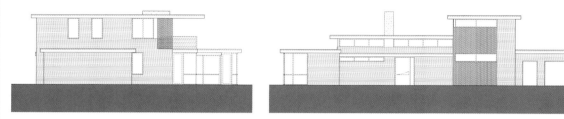

North elevation

East elevation

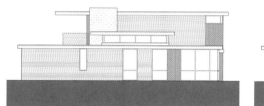

South elevation

West elevation

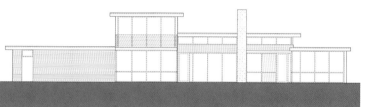

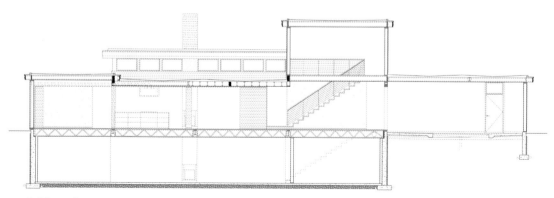

Building section

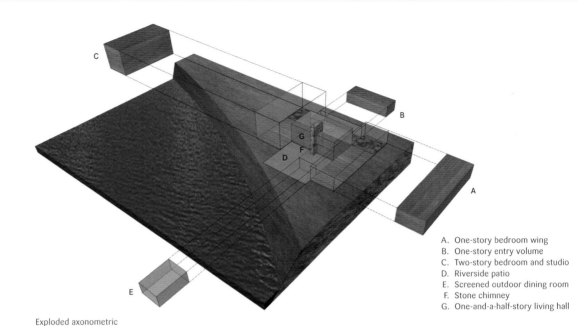

C

B

G
F
D

A

E

Exploded axonometric

A. One-story bedroom wing
B. One-story entry volume
C. Two-story bedroom and studio
D. Riverside patio
E. Screened outdoor dining room
F. Stone chimney
G. One-and-a-half-story living hall

O   O
H
N
P   N

Lower floor plan

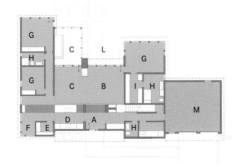

G   C   L   G
H
G   C   B   I   H
F   E   D   A   H   M

Main floor plan

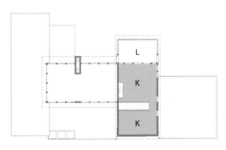

L
K
K

Upper floor plan

0   10   20 ft

N

A. Entry
B. Living room
C. Interior/exterior
   dining room
D. Kitchen
E. Pantry

F. Conservatory
G. Bedroom
H. Bathroom
I. Closet
J. Laundry room
K. Studio/library

L. Terrace/patio
M. Garage
N. Recreation room
O. Storage
P. Utilities

023

Like walls, built-in furniture can demarcate areas in a strong architectural way. Built-ins alone can define rooms, while fulfilling other functions through open or closed storage, seating, or surfaces such as tables, counters, and desks.

024

Built-ins promote the continuity of an open space containing different functions, and also ensure a smooth transition between them.

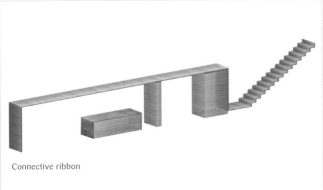

Connective ribbon

025

Bring outside materials to
the interior to emphasize the
indoor-outdoor connection.
Make sure that materials such
as wood and stone stand
out. This can be achieved by
displaying them in their most
natural way.

The glazing is engineered to reflect winter heat inward, while rejecting summer solar gain, and interior planes are positioned to display reflections of sunlight off the water.

This 2,218-square-foot home was designed to meet the rigorous requirements of Emerald Star certification developed by the Built Green residential building program. This program, aimed at providing environmental standards through efficient use of green technology, reclaimed materials, and renewable energy, awards an Emerald Star certification to those homes that reach a net-zero energy usage. This is an increasingly popular goal for green building, aimed at reducing energy demand to a minimum.

Emerald Star

Dwell Development

Seattle, Washington, United States

© Tucker English

The home's exterior siding is reclaimed Douglas fir and naturally weathered steel roofing panels from a cannery in Oregon's Willamette Valley. They also act as a protective rain screen.

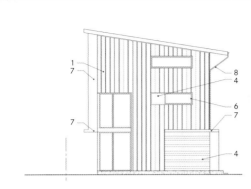

North (street) elevation

East elevation

South elevation

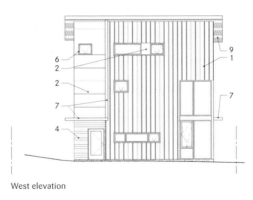

West elevation

1. Board and batten
2. Fiber cement panel color 1
3. Fiber cement panel color 2
4. Cedar siding
5. 36″ high rail 4″ max spacing
6. Vinyl window or door assembly
7. Framed canopy
8. Scupper and downspout
9. Cedar soffit

026

According to the National Renewable Energy Laboratory, a net-zero energy building is "a residential or commercial building with greatly reduced energy needs."

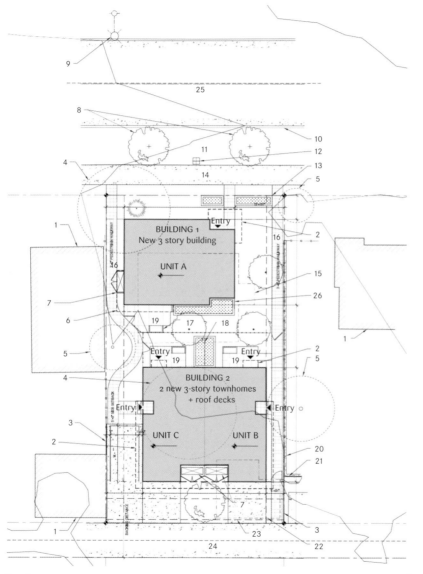

1. Existing structure
2. Canopy
3. Screen parking at side lot lines 5′0″ min height
4. Existing tree to be removed
5. Tree to remain
6. Framed canopy above
7. 6′x 2′ trash area
8. New street per landscape
9. Existing power pole
10. Existing 3.5″ rolled concrete curb
11. Existing planting strip
12. Existing water meter
13. Concrete planter per landscape
14. Existing concrete sidewalk
15. Existing structure to be removed
16. 3′0″ pedestrian walkway
17. Bench
18. Green screen per landscape
19. Patio
20. Existing concrete wall
21. Existing fence
22. Outline of existing structure to be removed
23. 1′0″ alley dedication
24. 10′0″ R.O.W. concrete paving
25. 66′0″ R.O.W. concrete paving
26. Bioretention planter

BUILDING 1
New 3 story building

UNIT A

BUILDING 2
2 new 3-story townhomes + roof decks

UNIT C   UNIT B

Entry

Site plan

N

Third floor plan

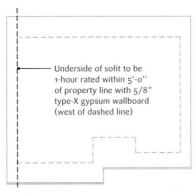

Underside of sofit to be
1-hour rated within 5'-0''
of property line with 5/8"
type-X gypsum wallboard
(west of dashed line)

Roof plan

Ground floor plan

Second floor plan

A. Entry
B. Storage
C. Powder room
D. Kitchen
E. Living area
F. Dining area
G. Bedroom
H. Washer/dryer
I. Mechanical room
J. Bathroom
K. Office
L. Master bedroom
M. Optional bedroom
N. Deck
O. Master bathroom
P. Walk-in-closet

027

A single-family home, labelled "Building 1," is part of a larger development that also includes a two-unit building. This project can be understood as urban infill, which is a planning tool that cities use in community redevelopment programs.

028

Mezzanines are a good design solution to make the most of spaces with very high ceilings, responding to a desire for compactness.

029

Mezzanines are versatile spaces that can accommodate from a comfortable sitting area to a functional home office. With no visual barriers other than a guardrail, mezzanines create a visual connection with the floor below.

Ninety percent of the wood used is reclaimed FSC-certified. That includes building framing, exterior paneling, and second-story flooring. The floors, stairs, and treads are built out of one-hundred-year-old hand-sewn mixed hardwoods from Montana, creating a stunning combination.

Countertops, cabinets, and tile made locally from high-recycled content contribute to the home's impressive inventory of eco-friendly materials.

U-House is the architect's own family residence and office. To accommodate the different functions, two new structures were built at each end of the property, both attached to a small industrial building already on site. The U shape of the house takes advantage of an open central space, protected from the surrounding urban setting. The walls framing the courtyard are punctuated with operable wood and glass panels, transforming this central space into another room of the house.

U-House

NDA
Natalie Dionne Architecture

Montreal, Quebec, Canada

© Marc Cramer, Katri Pyynönen

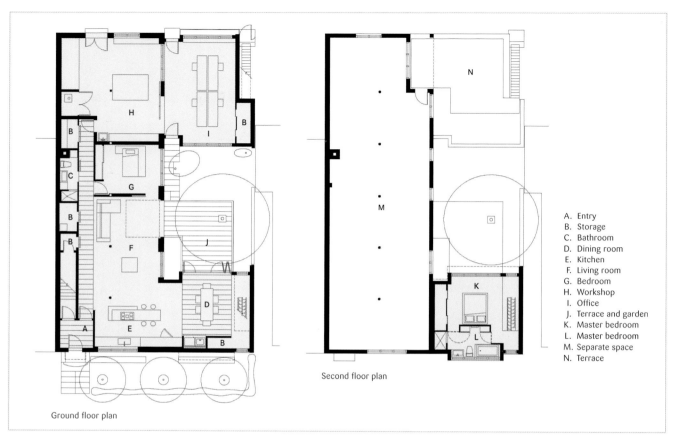

A. Entry
B. Storage
C. Bathroom
D. Dining room
E. Kitchen
F. Living room
G. Bedroom
H. Workshop
I. Office
J. Terrace and garden
K. Master bedroom
L. Master bedroom
M. Separate space
N. Terrace

Ground floor plan

Second floor plan

030

A central courtyard can be an important element of a house's organizational scheme. Protected by a surrounding building, a central courtyard can be used as an outdoor room for year-round comfort.

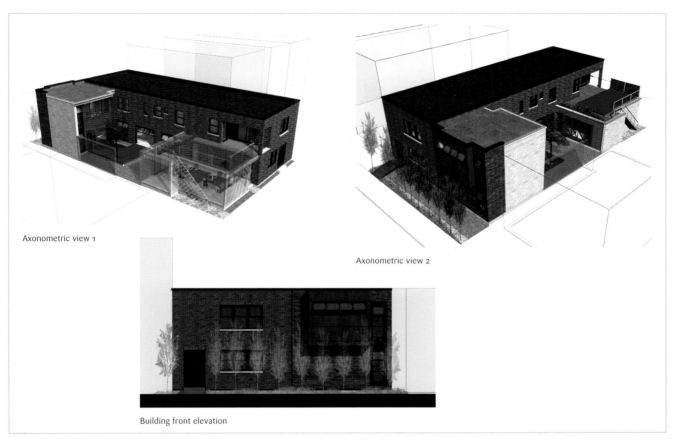

Axonometric view 1

Axonometric view 2

Building front elevation

From the street, the addition has its own identity, borrowing on the materiality of the existing buildings in the neighborhood. More particularly, it matches the height of the adjacent industrial building and echoes its simple and unadorned aesthetic.

031

A raised wood deck can enhance an outdoor space, demarcating a designated area for a specific function. The raised area can be conceived as an extension of an interior space if both floors—indoors and outdoors—are flush.

The various spaces in this residential
and office building are visually and
physically connected through the
central courtyard, which acts as
a gathering space, ensuring the
compatibility of the two environments.

The industrial aesthetic of the existing building permeates the addition, which uses an updated but familiar language that includes exposed wood joists, an aluminum ladder, and heavy-duty furnishings throughout.

032

Track lighting is a functional source for overall illumination as well as for task lighting. The variety of systems available can suit every look possible: one that blends with the overall design or one that stands out.

033

Garage doors need not only be used in garages. They offer an attractive alternative for indoor-outdoor transition to complement a home's industrial look.

The approach for the renovation and extension of the Hopetoun Road Residence embraces the client's desire to maintain the existing structure, strengthening the form with the creation of a gable façade at the front and back with a clearly defined outline. The façades are finished in polished gray stucco, emphasizing solidity and giving the house a reestablished sense of history and permanence. In contrast, the extensions, composed of ribbons of copper wrapping around the solid structure, sit softly above recessed glazing.

Hopetoun Road Residence

B.E Architecture

Melbourne, Victoria, Australia

© Peter Clarke

As a counterpoint to the verticality of the façade, the thin, single-level roofline expresses horizontality. The copper banding creates various spatial experiences as it interacts with the original house.

Second floor plan

Ground floor plan

The existing structure is retained as an
anchoring element to the architectural
language of the area, while a series
of pavilions are added underneath a
floating copper roofline that wraps
around the original building.

034

Pure geometric shapes and a limited palette of contrasting colors combine with the powerful effects of transparency to create a dynamic design that responds to the design principle of form follows function.

The tension and balance between old and new are carried into the interiors of the house. The existing structure maintains the intimate qualities of the original house, while prominent use of steel-framed windows is a unifying element throughout the project.

035

A color scheme composed of two contrasting colors like white and black can be warmed-up with the rich grain of wood to create a sharp, clean, yet welcoming kitchen.

The entry door is made of slices of agate instead of glass, using traditional leadlight techniques. Not only is it an artful complement to the minimalist furnishing approach of the entry hall, but it also concentrates the soul of the entire project: new meets old.

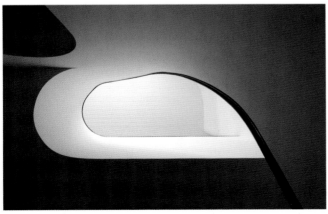

036

Using a monochromatic color scheme can dramatically enhance the special architectural features of a home. The color white allies with light to enliven a room with constantly changing shadow patterns.

The house is composed of a series of shed roof volumes offset to offer each major space stunning views of Mount Rainier across Lake Washington. The one- and two-story volumes overlap to create an airy, open plan, while a palette of white, black, and red combines with the clean geometric composition and exposed steel structure to give the building a crafted and enduring architectural quality.

The house boasts understated feng shui elements to direct the flow of the house, and to protect the kitchen as hearth. The lakeside of the house also opens up—via large pocket doors—to a covered outdoor dining area, perfect for gatherings.

HO Residence

CAST Architecture

Seattle, Washington, United States

© Dustin Peck Photography, Stefan Hampden/ Cast Architecture

037

An exterior wall with elements that create depth such as deep overhangs and balconies can protect interior spaces against the negative effects of direct sunlight such as glare and deterioration of some materials.

Building cross section

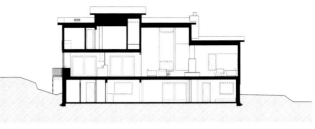

Building longitudinal section

0 5 10 ft

Upper floor plan

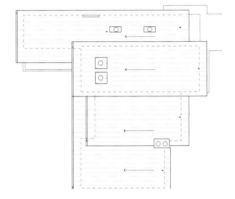

Roof plan

Lower floor plan

Main floor plan

A. Bedroom
B. Closet
C. Bathroom
D. Sitting area
E. Storage
F. Foyer
G. Powder room
H. Deck above
I. Entry
J. Mudroom
K. Den
L. Living room
M. Dining room
N. Deck
O. Kitchen
P. Garage
Q. Open to below
R. Master bedroom
S. Walk-in-closet
T. Roof deck
U. Master bathroom
V. Laundry room
W. Study

0 5 10 ft

N

038

The positioning of windows on various surfaces of different orientation and a palette of light colors offer an intermediate brightness between the windows and the interior surfaces.

039

Staircases can act as light shafts bringing daylight deep into a building. This effect is enhanced by open-tread stairs, which make the spaces around it look open and airy.

040

A combination of windows and skylights can balance a room's distribution of daylight, avoiding dark areas and glare.

While the design of the townhouse is unquestionably contemporary, the building relates to its classic Brooklyn context as an abstract reinterpretation of the classic brownstone townhouse, from the materiality of the zinc and custom concrete block to the alignment of the façade elements with neighboring buildings. As for the interior, the spaces are articulated to allow most efficient use of space, and to make the most of daylight and ventilation through large operable windows, balconies, and terraces. The design of the exterior areas of the house was as important as the interior portions.

State Street Townhouse

Ben Hansen Architect

Brooklyn, New York,
United States

© Francis Dzikowski
Photography

Generous outdoor spaces were provided, from play areas on the ground floor in the backyard, to more private and serene balconies and a planted roof deck. All these outdoor landscaped areas are harmoniously linked to their adjacent interior spaces.

The spaces have been arranged so that circulation is fluid, especially at the main level, where inhabitants can easily move between the kitchen, dining, and living rooms and have a visual and physical connection with the backyard.

Third floor plan

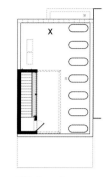

Fourth floor plan

Fifth floor plan

Basement floor plan

Ground floor plan

Second floor plan

A. Utility room
B. Storage
C. Front yard
D. Foyer
E. Bedroom
F. Bathroom
G. Playroom
H. Bar
I. Rear patio
J. Rear yard
K. Library
L. Living area
M. Dining area
N. Kitchen
O. Balcony
P. Laundry room
Q. Studio
R. Master shower
S. Master bathroom
T. Toilet
U. Walk-in-closet
V. Master bedroom
W. Balcony
X. Roof deck

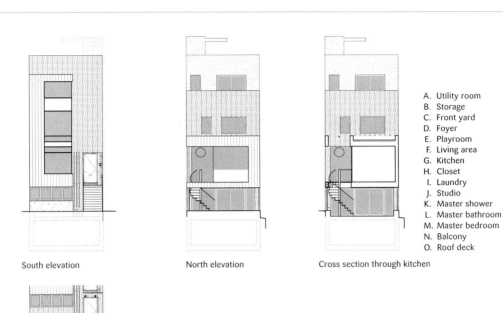

South elevation

North elevation

Cross section through kitchen

A. Utility room
B. Storage
C. Front yard
D. Foyer
E. Playroom
F. Living area
G. Kitchen
H. Closet
I. Laundry
J. Studio
K. Master shower
L. Master bathroom
M. Master bedroom
N. Balcony
O. Roof deck

Basement entry

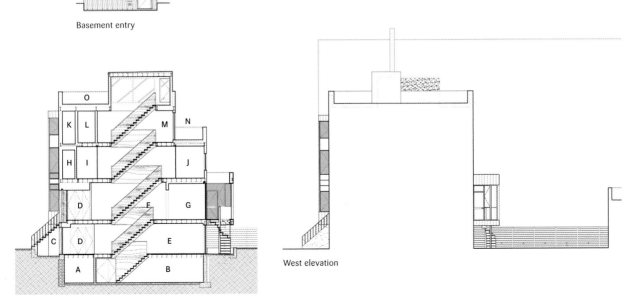

Building section

West elevation

041

If there is anything that
can make a big difference
to lifestyle and property
value it is an outdoor space,
whether a balcony, a terrace,
or a courtyard; the larger the
better, of course.

042

Generally, townhouses are long, narrow, and dark in the middle section. With only front and back walls as sources of light and ventilation, designers don't miss the opportunity to make these openings as big as possible.

043

Narrow dwellings bring spatial
challenges that lead designers
to minimize interior partitions
to optimize the use of space.
Since side walls have generally
no windows, the goal is to
bring light from the home's
front and back into the center.

044

It's always nice to provide rooms with large windows. But this design decision isn't simply aesthetic. Per code, all habitable rooms need to be provided with a glazed surface, whose area is a proportion of the room's square footage.

The rest of the floors are strictly defined by their own program and vertical circulations, allowing the most efficient way of space planning and making the most of natural light and ventilation through balconies, terraces, and large operable windows.

The scope of the project included the complete renovation of an existing 5,700-square-foot structure and 1,300 square feet of new construction. Also, the design of the home incorporated a dismantled nineteenth-century wood barn, whose different parts were transformed into new elements. Extensive landscape and hardscape improvements were integrated with the new design as well. A significant part of the design was intended to create a picturesque home entrance, with a decomposed granite path passing through a small grove of mature olive trees.

JK Home

Standard

Beverly Hills, California, United States

© Benny Chan

045

Double the impact with a
two-sided fireplace. One side
facing the interior, bringing
warmth and coziness, the
other facing the exterior,
transforming an ordinary
outdoor space into a true
extension of the home.

Floor plan

A. Entry
B. Den
C. Bathroom
D. Storage
E. Master bathroom
F. Hallway
G. Master bedroom
H. Living/dining area
I. Kitchen/breakfast nook
J. Laundry room
K. Bedroom

0   5   10   20 ft   N

046

The massing and geometry
of a building often expresses
the functional program of
its interior. "Form follows
function."

Large beams formed the entrance pavilion, siding was used for exterior cladding and interior ceilings, the maple granary for new doors, and the hardwood off-cuts were reassembled as an island top.

047

Glossy finishes absorb less light than those that are flat. When using a dark color in a room, a glossy finish will reflect light into an otherwise dim room.

048

Take your bathroom outdoors, and turn it into a stylish retreat blending privacy and affinity for nature, for instance.

The Glebe Residence is a 1,500-square-foot addition and full interior renovation to an existing 2,200-square-foot home for a family of outdoor enthusiasts. The existing two-story brick building, which was maintained, provides a direct historical reference to the urban environment, while a new third floor, subtly set back from the front façade and cantilevered along the north side of the existing building, forges new contextual relationships. The client's connection to the outdoors and the need to maintain an existing sugar maple tree were of key influence to the design.

Glebe Residence

Batay-Csorba Architects

Ottawa, Ontario, Canada
© Doublespace Photography

The rear massing strategy is guided by the limitations created by an existing sugar maple and the imposed site setbacks, creating a series of diagonally cantilevered masses.

049

Studies made at an early design stage allow for the exploration of volumetric, spatial, and programmatic relationships in order to provide a functional, comfortable, and aesthetically pleasing result.

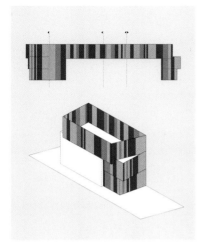

Diagram of exterior cladding

Volumetric study

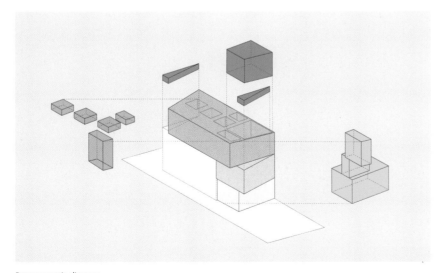

Programmatic diagram

The pivoting and cantilevered rear addition provides natural shading on the west-facing façade along with the existing mature tree. The north façade's thickened high-performance envelope has minimal openings, while the skylights and roof garden give maximum day lighting to the master suite.

Ground floor plan

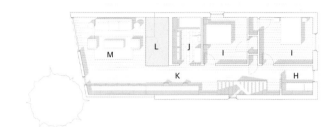

Ground floor plan

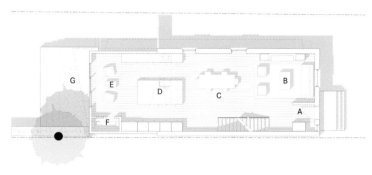

Ground floor plan

1 5 ft   N

A. Entry
B. Living room
C. Dining room
D. Kitchen
E. Sitting room
F. Powder room
G. Patio

H. Laundry room
I. Bedroom
J. Bathroom
K. Office
L. Open to below
M. Family room
N. Exercise room

O. Dressing room
P. Master bathroom
Q. Master bedroom
R. Light well
S. Master garden
   terrace
T. Open terrace

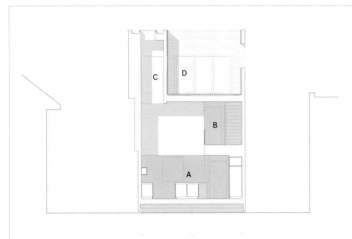

In the interior, the original Victorian typology is transformed by the insertion of a series of interconnected voids that create light shafts and visual relationships between rooms typically separated. Three-story voids also create a natural chimney effect for passive ventilation, which terminates with a series of solar-powered operable skylights.

A. Kitchen
B. Family room
C. Master bedroom beyond
D. Master garden terrace

Building cross section

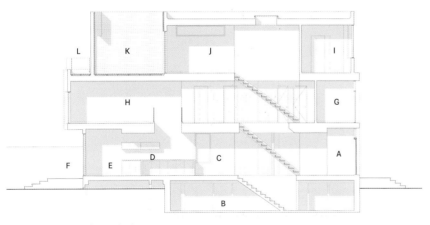

Building longitudinal section

1   5 ft

A. Entry
B. Basement
C. Dining room
D. Kitchen
E. Sitting room
F. Patio
G. Laundry room
H. Family room
I. Exercise room
J. Master bedroom
K. Master garden terrace
L. Open terrace

050

Clear or translucent dividers
define spaces, while allowing
light to filter. They add a layer
of complexity to a space,
creating exciting visual effects.

051

Make the most of a kitchen island, by turning it into a hub for multiple uses, such as for food preparation, storage, and dining.

052

Voids between floors create vertical relationships, extending visual reach and creating a sense of amplitude. Staircases, double-height spaces, and mezzanines are some examples.

The new internal voids through the house provide for passive ventilation, creating an internal chimney effect, which draws warm air up three stories to four solar-powered operable north-facing skylights with automated sun control devices.

053

Opening up the bathroom
to an adjacent bedroom is
a good space-saving solution.
By eliminating any partition
between the two areas,
sources of natural light
can reach deep into the
shared space.

On the third floor the master suite extends to the exterior via two distinctive terraces. The first is conceived as an introverted private space secluded from direct engagement with adjacent properties by nine-foot-high walls. The second is a sliver of deck that provides unobstructed views of the property.

The house is named "Link" in reference to the last vacant parcel in the neighborhood where it now stands: the missing link. Its form was generated by abstracting the common scale, form, and massing of the original houses in the historic district in response to the requirements of the City of Phoenix Historic Preservation Committee. This resulted in the creation of a simple massing diagram: a social open living box, and a box for the utility components of the home. While most house designs tend to be closed to the street and open to their private backyards, the Link House is connected to both.

Link House

The Ranch Mine

Phoenix, Arizona, United States

© Jason + Anna Photography

Huge sliding glass doors enable the entire living space to become an open-air pavilion, extending the living area outdoors to the private backyard and social front porch.

Deep overhangs shade the glass doors in the summer and the doors provide ideal cross-ventilation during the cool desert nights. LED lighting, advanced framing, and only north-south windows help to keep this house incredibly energy efficient.

Massing diagram

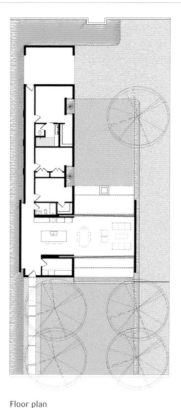

Floor plan

054

The structure of a building can, in some cases, define areas where different activities take place, optimizing planning and articulating circulation paths. For instance, the Link House's structure clearly differentiates social and utility functions.

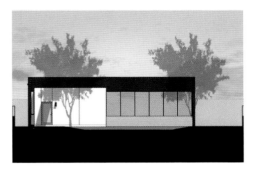

South elevation

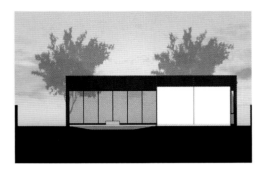

North elevation

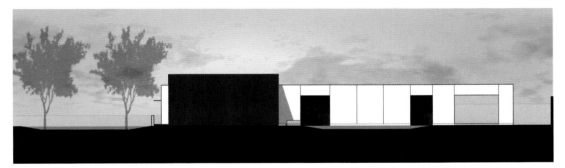

East elevation

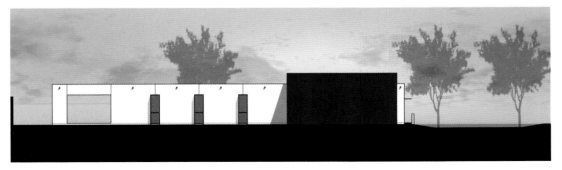

West elevation

055

Sliding doors on opposite walls can turn a room into a sheltered outdoor space, recalling the basic principles of natural passive airflow. It's all about capturing natural breezes and directing them to flow through a room.

Standard developer-grade materials including concrete floors, quartz countertops, and walnut millwork were selected for their low-maintenance qualities and were used in a unique, modern way.

The Showhouse explores new materials, tests new construction techniques, and ensures the functionality of new forms. While employing innovative design methods throughout, the home engages with the surrounding neighborhood through its form, exterior materials, and its two-and-a-half-story proportion. The Showhouse is a contemporary take on a traditional building form with limestone, brick, cedar siding, ornamental ironwork, and a landscape design that focuses on native grasses.

Showhouse

Hufft Projects

Kansas City, Missouri,
United States

© Mike Sinclair, Hufft Projects

Despite its fifty-foot-wide lot, the house has an airy, open feel. This was achieved through the use of skylights and the creation of smart space dividers that make the most of the space available.

A. Front porch
B. Dining room
C. Powder room
D. Foyer
E. Kitchen
F. Mudroom
G. Living room
H. Porte-cochère
I. Back porch
J. Playroom
K. Kids' bedroom
L. Laundry room
M. Kids' bathroom
N. Balcony
O. Study
P. Dressing room
Q. Master bathroom
R. Toilet
S. Master bedroom

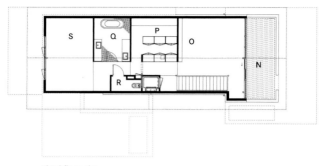

Third floor plan

Second floor plan

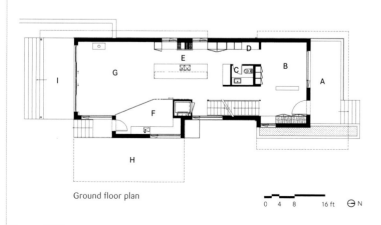

Ground floor plan

0 4 8   16 ft   N

056

The natural finish of certain materials, including wood, stone, and even tarnished metal, as shown in this image, imbues a room a unique look.

057

A one-wall kitchen combined with an island works like a galley kitchen, with the difference that the combination doesn't comprise an enclosed room. The island adds work surface or seating for informal meals.

058

Creativity and color can transform a dull space into a room a kid would want to spend time in. Paint, tilework, and decorative wall decals are an easy, cost-effective design solution.

059

Skylights above staircases are
convenient to filter light down
to lower floors. If operable,
they will draw warm air from
the floors below through
the roof.

The master bedroom on the third floor is conceived as a tranquil retreat separated from the other rooms of the house. It shares the mostly open plan with the master bathroom, a dressing room, and a study with access to a balcony.

This project tackles the full-scale renovation of a Victorian home making the most of its high location with views to the San Francisco skyline. The design transforms a classic Victorian dwelling into a hybrid of vintage and modern style, satisfying the requirements of a contemporary lifestyle through the open feel of the renovation and the use of vintage touches that connect past and present. As a result, steel elements and geometric shapes coexist with the classic features of the original Victorian base.

Victorian House Remodel

Floriana Interiors

San Francisco, California, United States

© Judy Reed, Steph Dewey

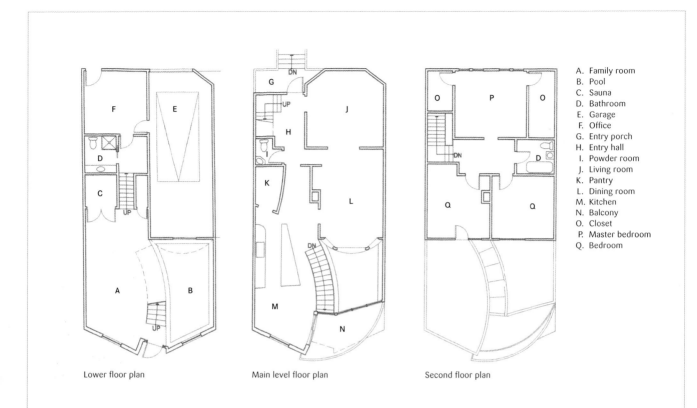

Lower floor plan

Main level floor plan

Second floor plan

A. Family room
B. Pool
C. Sauna
D. Bathroom
E. Garage
F. Office
G. Entry porch
H. Entry hall
I. Powder room
J. Living room
K. Pantry
L. Dining room
M. Kitchen
N. Balcony
O. Closet
P. Master bedroom
Q. Bedroom

The remodel of this Victorian
row house opens up an originally
compartmentalized layout,
making circulation more fluid and
interconnecting spaces—especially
on the main level.

060

Mirrors amplify the perception of a room, making it look larger than it actually is. Mirrors are also tools to magnify the amount of light in a room, especially when combined with light-colored surfaces.

061

The curved metal stair is a central architectural element in this house. It opens it up, transforming a once-dark dwelling into a light-filled home, thanks to the open staircase, the large windows, and the skylight.

062

The atmosphere of a home's interior can be influenced by its relationship with the exterior. Whether it's a backyard, a terrace, or a balcony, an outdoor space enlivens a home.

An old 1930s Magic Chef stove juxtaposes the feeling of the airy space with its exposed I-beams, steel, and glass. The pantry is tucked behind the curved wall decorated with the nostalgic vintage metal billboard.

Located in a residential neighborhood in midtown Toronto, this house qualifies as an infill. The design process, which involved lengthy discussions with the owner, neighbors, community design groups, and city officials, mainly focused on the look of the house, especially the shape and height of the roof.

The design embraces the iconic, house-like forms in the existing streetscape and reinforces the setbacks, materials, and relationship with grade. In order to match existing massing on the street, a new third floor is set back at the front and rear, providing opportunities for green roof terraces.

Moore Park Residence

Drew Mandel Architects
Toronto, Ontario, Canada
© Ben Rahn / A-Frame

The house forms a complex mass-
to-void composition. It is structured
by a board-formed concrete wall, a
large light well, transparent partitions,
and interconnecting void spaces.
The basement opens out to a narrow
courtyard, which is open to light
from above.

Cross section A   Longitudinal section

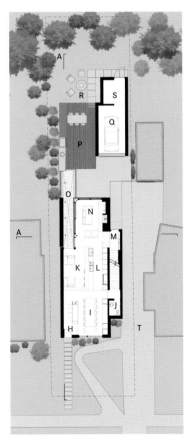

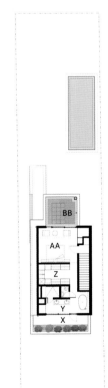

A. Laundry room
B. Bathroom
C. Wine cellar
D. Media room
E. Mechanical room
F. Fitness studio
G. Office
H. Entry
I. Dining area
J. Powder room
K. Lounge
L. Kitchen
M. Rear entry
N. Living room
O. Light well
P. Deck
Q. Garage
R. Fire pit
S. Storage
T. Mutual drive
U. Bedroom
V. Family room
W. Green roof
X. Terrace
Y. Master bathroom
Z. Walk-in-closet
AA. Master bedroom
BB. Green roof terrace

Basement floor plan

Site and ground floor plan

Second floor plan

Third floor plan

N

The boundary between building interior and exterior is dematerialized. The spaces are visually interconnected, yet defined for varied activities of modern family living.

063

There is perhaps no other room in the house that benefits more from natural light than the kitchen, which requires both ambient and task lighting. An adequate number of light fixtures makes up for the lack of natural light at night.

064

Building regulations require that certain openings in exterior walls be fire-protected. Because the south wall of the house is so close to the property line, a firewall was required in order to allow for unrated windows on that side.

The third floor accommodates a master suite that enjoys private roof terraces on the east and west ends of the house that offer delightful views of the tree canopy in the neighborhood. The third floor is set back from the front and rear of the house in order to match existing massing of the neighboring houses and streetscape.

Built on a wide, yet very shallow lot, House 3 sits against its western neighbor and opens onto its eastern side to create a private fenced courtyard. The black siding expresses a modern and warm, clean and welcoming aesthetic. On the other hand, the texture of the wood grain complements more traditional neighboring houses. The plan is simple and flexible, to allow for the changing needs of the owners. This is a result of a design process that considers the flow between spaces and levels, and the opportunities to create connections between the interior and the landscape.

House 3 (H3)

MODERNest

Toronto, Ontario, Canada

© Steven Evans

Natural wood accents are revealed where the rectangular volume is carved away to create recessed entry porches, shaded exterior decks, and windows.

Second floor plan

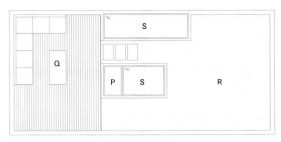

Roof plan

Basement floor plan

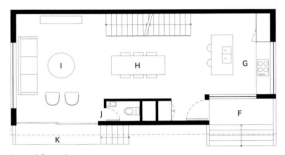

Ground floor plan

A. Guestroom
B. Bathroom
C. Rec room
D. Storage
E. Utility room
F. Front entry
G. Kitchen
H. Dining room
I. Living room
J. Powder room

K. Side deck
L. Master bedroom
M. En suite bathroom
N. Den
O. Laundry
P. Roof access
Q. Roof terrace
R. Green roof
S. Skylight

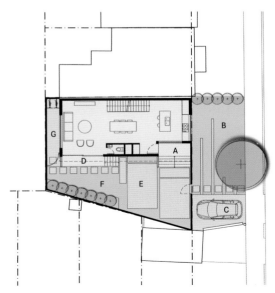

Site plan

N

A. Front entry
B. Front yard
C. Parking
D. Side deck
E. Outdoor dining
F. Side yard
G. Storage

The dark exterior is in contrast with the bright white interior, which is designed to capture as much daylight as possible, given the building code restrictions on windows in walls along lot lines.

The house incorporates large skylight
elements, generous windows up to the
ceiling, and access to exterior spaces.

065

A freestanding tub is a focal point in any bathroom, transforming a traditionally utilitarian room into a personal and nurturing spa-like space, where well-being and design go arm-in-arm.

Veranda House is a single-family home located in a new forest development. It is designed to be intimate and discreet, with few openings facing the street. Instead, the house opens up to a secluded backyard through large openings on the ground floor that ease the connection between interior and exterior spaces, and large windows that embrace the surrounding landscape. The focus on the natural environment is emphasized by the neutral selection of materials: clay brick, cedar, and glass.

Veranda House

Blouin Tardif Architecture-Environnement

Boucherville, Quebec, Canada

© Steve Monpetit

On the south side, the house makes the most of the ample private space surrounding the veranda. The heart of the house is a series of spaces that open onto the yard: the kitchen, dining room, and double-height living room.

066

The slope of a shed roof has a significant design impact on the exterior of a house. The different inclines of the roof allow for the creation of two opposite elevations that relate differently to the surroundings.

Second floor plan

067

The L-shape configuration embraces outdoor areas to which interior spaces can be directly connected. While creating a private courtyard, this configuration acts as a protecting screen against prevailing winds.

A. Entry
B. Cloakroom
C. Powder room
D. Wine cellar
E. Pantry
F. Kitchen
G. Dining room
H. Living room
I. Mechanical room
J. Bicycle parking
K. Garage
L. Storage
M. Family room
N. Bathroom
O. Porch
P. Terrace
Q. Pool
R. Shed
S. BBQ
T. Office
U. Bedroom
V. Laundry room
W. Master bedroom
X. Master bathroom
Y. Walk-in-closet
Z. Green roof

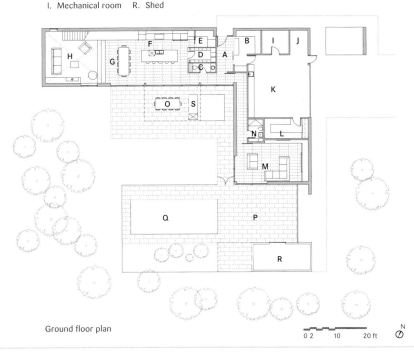

Ground floor plan

0 2   10   20 ft

N

068

A careful selection of
materials and a high level of
craftsmanship can enhance a
simple, minimalist architecture.

The use of wood in the kitchen and dining area combines with a low ceiling to create an intimate space, in contrast with the cool white, light-filled living area, which transmits a sense of openness thanks to the high ceiling.

069

Large sliding doors allow interior and exterior spaces to blend, as does a continuous floor covering. Wood ceilings give rooms an outdoorsy feel.

070

An LED channel mounted to the underside of a handrail makes an interesting visual effect. Light strips with adhesive backing can easily achieve this effect, but wiring might be a little tricky and ways of hiding it would have to be explored.

On the second floor, the master bedroom features an en suite bathroom with transparent partitions and a large covered deck resembling an aerie facing the woods and the water below.

The East Van House is located on an atypical fifty by seventy-five-feet lot with no back road access, as opposed to the standard thirty-three by one-hundred-and-twenty-feet lot, that backs onto a schoolyard. The neighborhood is eclectic, with streetscapes that reflect the diversity of the community.

The house is designed with a dominant asymmetrical geometry to comply with the prescriptive zoning requirements for the area. While the two-bedroom house is tailored for a single professional, an open office is roughed-in for a bathroom and planned for an easy conversion into a third bedroom on the upper floor.

East Van House

Splyce Design

Vancouver, British Columbia, Canada

© Ivan Hunter

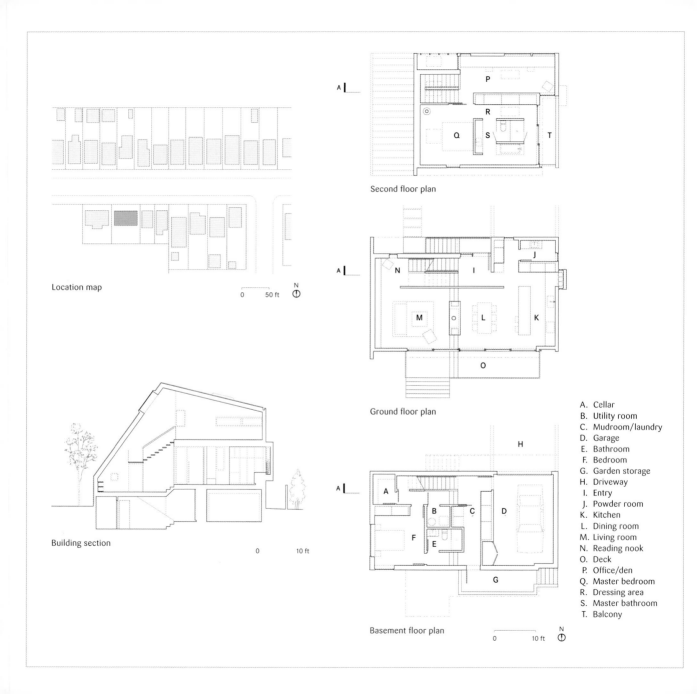

Location map

0   50 ft   N

Second floor plan

P

R

Q   S   T

A

Ground floor plan

N   I

J

M   L   K

O

A

Building section

0   10 ft

Basement floor plan

H

A

B   C   D

F   E

G

A

0   10 ft   N

A. Cellar
B. Utility room
C. Mudroom/laundry
D. Garage
E. Bathroom
F. Bedroom
G. Garden storage
H. Driveway
I. Entry
J. Powder room
K. Kitchen
L. Dining room
M. Living room
N. Reading nook
O. Deck
P. Office/den
Q. Master bedroom
R. Dressing area
S. Master bathroom
T. Balcony

071

A room with three solid sides and its fourth formed by sliding glass doors can be turned into a porch or semi-outdoor room during good weather, expanding its area and spilling its functions outside.

072

Built-in furniture can be designed to double as space dividers, optimizing the use of space and integrating with the architectural envelope that contains it.

Windows on this side face the street and are decidedly small to ensure privacy. A low window, at the widened main floor stair landing, is carefully calibrated, so one sitting in the adjoining library can gain discreet views out.

073

A simple interior palette of materials and white walls allow for dynamic plays of light and shadow throughout the day.

074

Skylights are sized and located to avoid views to and from neighbors and allow natural light to penetrate deep into parts of a house that could otherwise not benefit from it.

Similarly, sliding glass doors in the master bathroom extend the shower and tub space onto a private, cedar-screened deck, enhancing the spa-like experience.

Located in an area undergoing reinvention from its industrial heritage, this new house replaces a nondescript workers cottage that was substantially altered. Its frontage establishes a strong contextual response to the traditional but diverse neighborhood in a clearly contemporary architectural composition, maintaining the prevailing street line. The home is organized around three courtyards linked along a circulation axis. Only from the central courtyard are its three stories fully revealed.

Alexandria Courtyard House

Matthew Pullinger Architect

Sydney, New South Wales, Australia

© Brett Boardman Photography

075

An operable screen system provides sun protection against direct sunlight and allows control of privacy levels, while significantly changing the appearance of a building's elevation.

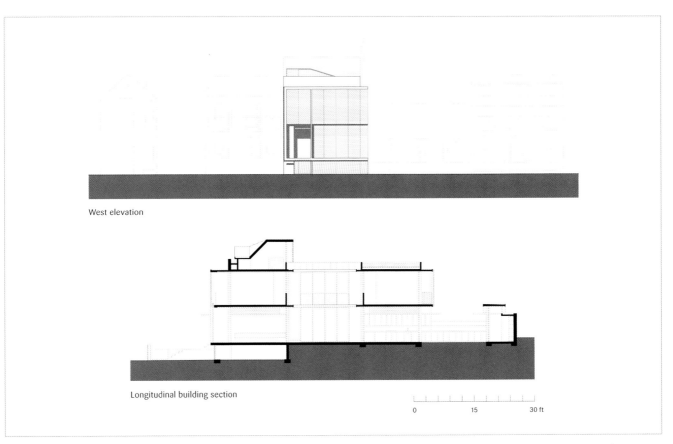

West elevation

Longitudinal building section

0   15   30 ft

The house matches the northern, attached neighbor's parapet height and alignment to then sit strongly framed within the streetscape. A third floor is folded within a steel-wrapped roof form, set behind the concrete parapet, receding from the street view.

The clean, generously proportioned interiors exude a sense of calm and space, offering a peaceful retreat from the tumult of the surrounding city. Restrained detailing hides the clutter of modern life, with all unsightly appliances and devices concealed.

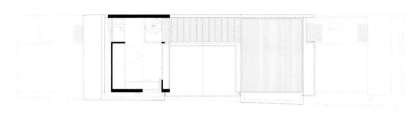

Third floor plan

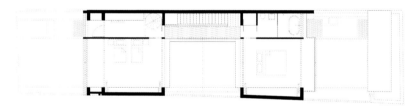

Second floor plan

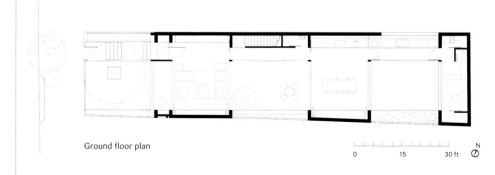

Ground floor plan

0   15   30 ft

N

076

Interior courtyards are excellent ideas for the creation of intimate outdoor areas. They also act as efficient space organizers, separating the different functions of a home into different areas.

077

Sliding doors around courtyards offer a high degree of flexibility, expanding interior living spaces to the exterior, or compartmentalizing these spaces without affecting circulation.

At ground level, operable floor-to-ceiling glass doors demarcate the courtyards. Carefully resolved and detailed, there are no thresholds or bulkheads, leaving clean floor and ceiling planes.

The design deploys traditional construction techniques and materials, with a rugged industrial aesthetic, class-one off-form concrete, weathered unfinished timber, face brick, and galvanized steel.

The environmental qualities of the site are used as inspiration for the design to create a sense of place. The Mojave landscape maintains an inherent beauty of textures, stratifications, and materials as well as protected oasis of color brought to life under the play of shadow patterns of a harsh sun. Tresarca has been developed around a simple expression of forms and materials. Separated into functions, the forms create opportunities for protected courtyards, and cross-circulation. Composition, materiality compatibility, and clarity of construction also played a large part in the design.

Tresarca

assemblageSTUDIO

Las Vegas, Nevada,
United States

© Bill Timmerman,
Zack Hussain

078

Circulation paths should be designed not as residual spaces as a result of a room planning approach, but rather as an integral aspect of the whole design, one that connects rooms, guides occupants, and enhances the spatial experience.

079

Outdoor spaces are designed to fulfill specific functions, but they also need to be understood as complementary parts of interior space, and as connectors of different blocks, composing a home.

Space is not determined by enclosure, but through a new idea of space extending past perceived barriers into an expanded form of living inside and outside. Even in the harsh environment, one is able to enjoy this concept through the succession of exterior courts, which are designed to shade and protect.

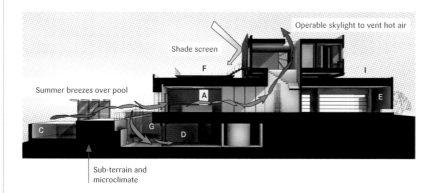

Operable skylight to vent hot air

Shade screen

Summer breezes over pool

Sub-terrain and microclimate

Functions as a barrier from radiant heat gain, ultimately, creating air circulation and contributing to passive cooling.

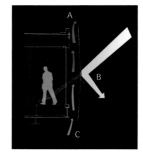

Section through screen

A. Heat chimney
B. Light diffraction
C. Fresh air

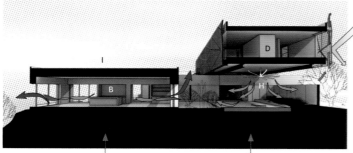

A. Living/kitchen
B. Pool house
C. Pool
D. Bedroom
E. Garage
F. Roof deck
G. Lower courtyard
H. Entry
I. Roof garden

Large sliders for passive cooling

Air circulation and evaporative cooling

Sections

The mesh screen provides a protection from the harsh sun on the interior spaces. An analysis of the desert floor and nearby red rock mountain formations gave inspiration to the mesh screen, which became an important juxtaposition to the simple rectilinear forms hidden beyond.

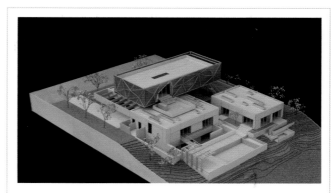

Scale model

Second floor plan

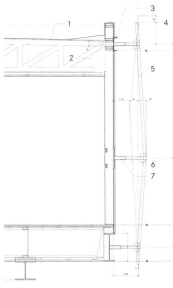

Typical attachment details

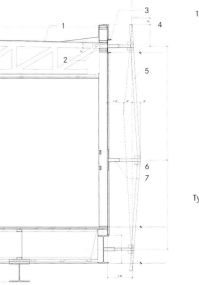

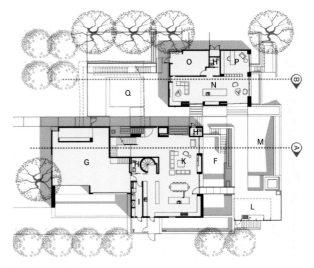

Ground floor plan

Typical attachment section

1. Single plywood membrane over plywood deck per structural drawings
2. 3/8" bent steel plate per structural drawings
3. Continuous flashing at top and bottom of continuous C channel 10 x 15.3"
4. New mesh height, align with top of parapet

5. 3-1/2" x 3-1/2" x 1/4"
6. 3/8" plate steel fin, angles vary per elevations
7. 3-1/2" diameter pipe
8. Wood truss
9. 7/8" plaster over waterproof membrane over plywood
10. Flashing
11. Weld per structural drawings
12. 6 x 12" wood post

Basement

⊖ N

A. Living/Kitchen area
B. Mechanical room
C. Storage
D. Bedroom
E. Bathroom
F. Lower courtyard
G. Garage
H. Powder room

I. Laundry room
J. Kitchen/dining area
K. Living area
L. BBQ area
M. Pool
N. Pool house. Living area
O. Pool house. Studio
P. Pool house. Office

Q. Entry
R. Master bedroom
S. Master bathroom
T. Dressing room
U. Walk-in-closet
V. Lounge
W. Roof deck
X. Roof garden

The center of the home is the great room. It is the centralizing connector to the other spaces of the home, the area where occupants come together and conduct social activities. It has the potential to act as a pass-through to all other areas of the home: pool house, bedrooms, lower level, multiple courts, and pool deck.

080

From an aesthetic standpoint, materials can define spaces, providing them with identity. From a conceptual standpoint, they may take cue from the surrounding environment, facilitating the contextual integration of the built work.

The Brown Residence celebrates the surrounding desert landscape with a design of simple stucco volumes that play against steel and glass. The careful configuration of the house blocks out the views of neighboring houses and instead focuses on distant mountain views. While the front of the residence presents an unassuming, modest scale, it descends the sloping site in a series of stepped blocks, forming generous interior spaces. Courtyards planted with native, drought-resistant plants and walkways articulate these blocks to subtly merge with the expansive desert landscape.

Brown Residence

Lake|Flato Architects

Scottsdale, Arizona, United States

© Bill Timmerman

081

Design vocabulary should leverage the topography, the landscape, and the climate where construction takes place, following sustainable practices in order to minimize the use of resources and the environmental impact.

Oversize pivot doors and large expanses of glass allow abundant light and air into the spaces, while broad overhangs and shading devices protect them from the harsh desert sun.

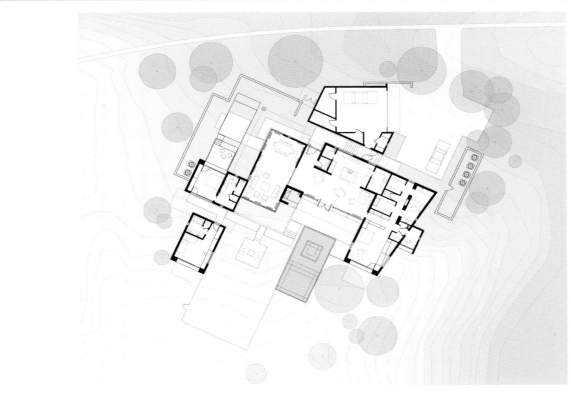

Floor plan

082

The optimal orientation
ensures that a building is
positioned in relation to
the sun's path and the wind
patterns in order to optimize
energy efficiency and comfort.

083

Pivot doors are a dramatic
and modern alternative
to common swing doors.
Detailing that involves pivot
doors is generally cleaner,
because pivot doors don't
require door frames, as
opposed to swing doors.

While mainly glass, the clever placement of opaque enclosures allows the occupants of the house to freely enjoy the surrounding landscape, while feeling their privacy protected.

The concrete and stone landscape design defines all exterior spaces around the house. Concrete continues inside as the predominant floor material, while natural wood provides warmth on various wall, ceiling, and floor surfaces throughout the house.

Bm Modular One is composed of thirteen modules and was built in two weeks. The foundation and basement were constructed with polished concrete floors on-site, while the modules were fabricated off-site, then shipped on flatbeds to the building location, where they were assembled within two days.

The massing provides opportunities to combine several exterior materials so that the house can be adapted to different environments. Both modern and filled with light, the house employs all of the intended benefits of modular building without compromising proportion, light, scale, and texture.

bm Modular One

Robert M. Gurney, Architect

Bethesda, Maryland,
United States

© Maxwell MacKenzie,
David Burroughs

084

The proportion of glass-to-solid
in a building's walls needs to
respond to site conditions
and to orientation in order
to achieve good thermal
performance.

085

Add stylish touches to your outdoor spaces that will increase your property value. The style of your landscape design should complement that of your house to create a unified whole.

The house employs repeatable parts that can be combined into custom configurations and brings together durable corrugated metal siding with stucco and Spanish cedar.

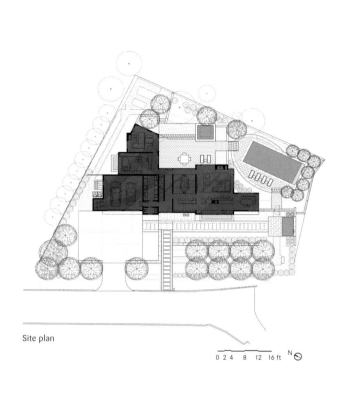

Site plan

0 2 4 8 12 16 ft N

Second floor plan

Ground floor plan

Basement floor plan

0 2 4 8 12 16 ft N

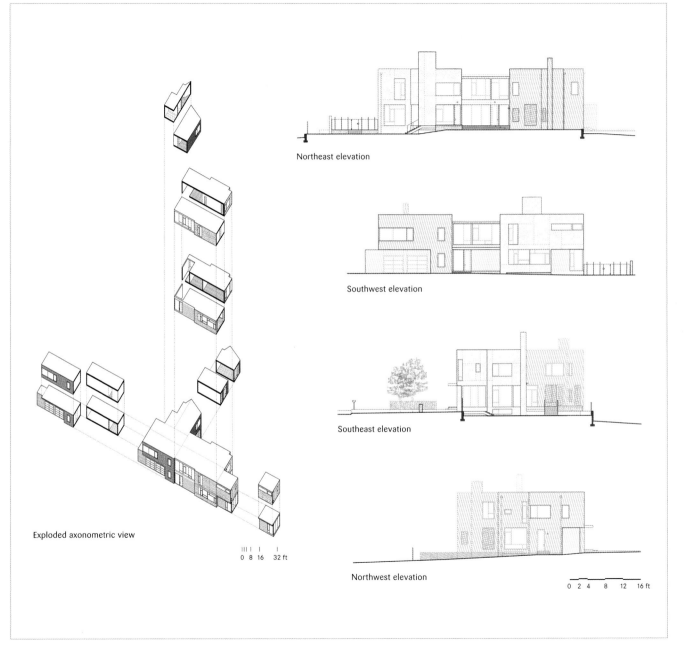

Exploded axonometric view

||| | |
0 8 16   32 ft

Northeast elevation

Southwest elevation

Southeast elevation

Northwest elevation

0 2 4   8   12   16 ft

A geothermal HVAC system and tight, super-insulated, exterior floor, wall, and roof systems pair with carefully specified finishes to achieve a high energy-efficient home with comfortable interiors.

Interior finishes include maple flooring, walnut millwork, aluminum stairs, and other materials specific to the client's preferences, while large expanses of glass are designed to allow for varying orientations.

086

Glass guardrails provide a way to enhance a home interior without sacrificing safety. Although it may seem fragile, the thick glass used for the construction is very resistant, making breakage unlikely to happen.

087

The design flexibility that glass walls allow is limitless. Technical requirements hardly get in the way of creating glass walls that allow architects and designers to play with the grid, and with different mullion thicknesses.

088

Clerestory windows allow natural light into a room without compromising privacy. They also don't occupy valuable wall space, where you can put a piece of furniture or hang a mirror.

The design of this house responds to a family's search for space without having to leave what had been their neighborhood for the past thirty years. This neighborhood is characterized by old trees and large plots that have a limited relationship with the street. The house, which replaces an old building, has an H shape, adapting to the presence of significant trees on the property. This shape creates various courtyards that harness the presence of these trees.

Fray Léon House

57STUDIO
Santiago, Chile
© Guy Wenborne

089

Courtyards are conceived as extensions of the house that seem to dematerialize as a way to ease the integration of the built work into the natural environment.

Windows create breaks in the building's
walls, creating dynamic elevations.
These breaks emphasize the points
where the wings of the house intersect.

The presence of significant trees in the property conditioned the house design. Access to the house is through a south-oriented courtyard with a Chilean acorn. The north courtyard has a large avocado tree, and the private spaces wing opens up to the eastern side of the property, where stand an old cypress Macrocarpa and some crape myrtles.

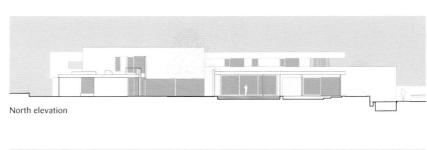

North elevation

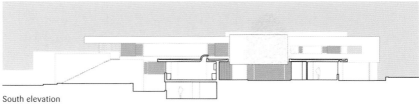

South elevation

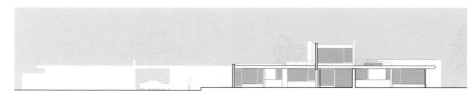

East elevation

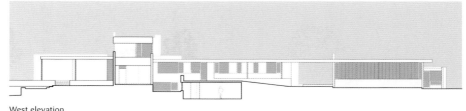

West elevation

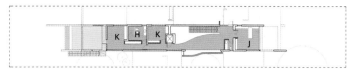

Second floor plan

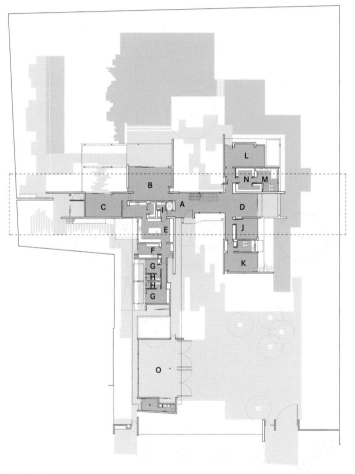

Ground floor plan

A. Hall
B. Living room
C. Dining room
D. Family room
E. Kitchen
F. Laundry room
G. Maid's room
H. Bathroom
I. Powder room
J. Office
K. Bedroom
L. Master bedroom
M. Master bathroom
N. Dressing room
O. Garage

0 1   5   10 mts   N

090

Plants and shrubs soften the rigid structure of a paved outdoor space, fostering the integration between architecture and nature.

091

Interior spaces with few partitions promote flexibility and adaptability to accommodate different functions, facilitate circulation between different areas, and offer extended sightlines, enhancing the spatial experience.

092

Properly placed windows can aid in energy savings, while windows that are not appropriately placed can lead to high energy use, and discomfort due to glare.

The sinuous opening of the staircase on
the second level softens the orthogonal
layout of the house and echoes the
undulating wall over the entry.

T House sits in a forest clearing, high up in a hillside, offering beautiful views to rolling agricultural valleys and distant mountains. The house is composed of two blocks in a green field. One is a two-story cubic structure clad with wood. The other is a single-story rectangular volume, covered with composite cement panels. The latter is buried into the ground at one end and cantilevered over the hill at the other end. The two structures are subtly linked by a glass structure, so as not to weaken the strong geometries of the two blocks.

T House

NDA
Natalie Dionne Architecture

Sutton, Quebec, Canada

© Marc Cramer

093

The simple geometric composition of the house and the use of materials—wood and cement panels—provide a harmonious contrast and a textural balance to the natural surroundings.

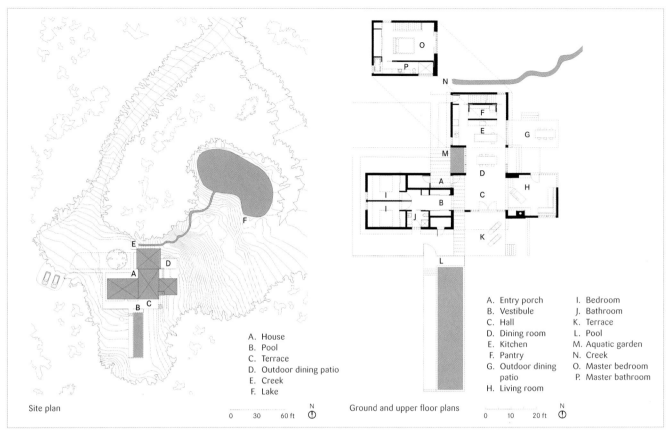

A. House
B. Pool
C. Terrace
D. Outdoor dining patio
E. Creek
F. Lake

Site plan

0   30   60 ft   N ⊕

A. Entry porch
B. Vestibule
C. Hall
D. Dining room
E. Kitchen
F. Pantry
G. Outdoor dining
   patio
H. Living room
I. Bedroom
J. Bathroom
K. Terrace
L. Pool
M. Aquatic garden
N. Creek
O. Master bedroom
P. Master bathroom

Ground and upper floor plans

0   10   20 ft   N ⊕

Taking cues from its bucolic environment, this architecture is defined and modulated by the natural views, the sunlight, and the topography of the site. The house, its gardens, terraces, and swimming pool foster a cruciform plan oriented along the north-south and east-west axes.

Finishing details are the soul of the house. Exterior wall finishes of torrefied wood, cement board, Cor-Ten steel, and white oak paneling penetrate the interior, while continuity of horizontal surfaces in concrete, limestone, and slate blur the boundaries between outside and inside.

094

Fenestration should be applied as a function of climate and orientation to ensure the comfort of each space in winter as well as in summer.

Built-in furniture is designed with attention to detail and executed with precision, whether it's the fireplace, the bookshelves in the living room, or the kitchen furniture with its floating island apron.

095

Concrete and natural stone flooring preserve freshness in summer; exposed to direct sunlight and equipped with a hydronic heating system, they provide ideal comfort during the cold seasons.

The home's lighting makes the place enchanting at night. General recessed lighting throughout the space is complemented with light fixtures carefully aimed at specific areas: efficient task lighting in the kitchen and track lighting directed to the bookshelf and wall art.

096

If room allows, putting a bed in the middle of a bedroom can be a good idea. The headboard can become a central piece, doubling as a chest of drawers, a bookshelf, or simply a plain, finished surface.

Surrounded by golf courses and fields of natural landscape, the project seeks to incorporate its surroundings into the house, as part of a design experience, following the client's desire to spend as much time as possible outside.

The site has a park to the north and streets to the west and south. The house is placed close to the intersection of the two streets, with the main access located on the south side. By placing the house at one end of the property, space is left for a garden, creating continuity with the park and clearing the views toward the Andes.

Kübler House

57STUDIO

Las Brisas de Chicureo, Colina, Chile

© Guy Wenbourne

The northeast corner of the property is framed by a barbecue area with a pool. The garden is the link between this separate area and the house.

A reflecting pool along the east wall guides the path from the entry, across the patio, the covered terrace, and the garden beyond. The juxtaposition of the reflecting pool against the tall wall reinforces the perspective through the patio.

All the interior spaces are organized around a twenty-six-feet-square central patio that concentrates the essence of the surrounding landscape. Demarcated by the roof, the patio opens its north face to frame the view toward the garden.

The public areas constantly interact with the central patio, while the service areas are tucked in the southwest corner of the house, keeping sightlines unobstructed. The private areas on the east side are clearly demarcated by a two-story-tall wall that blocks physical connection with the courtyard but maintains a visual link through an opening on the ground floor between the reflecting pool and the staircase.

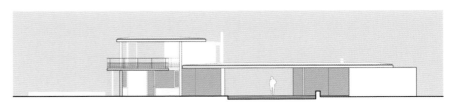

North elevation

East elevation

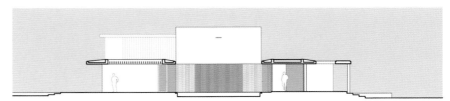

North-South building section

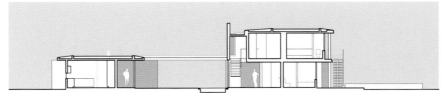

West-East building section

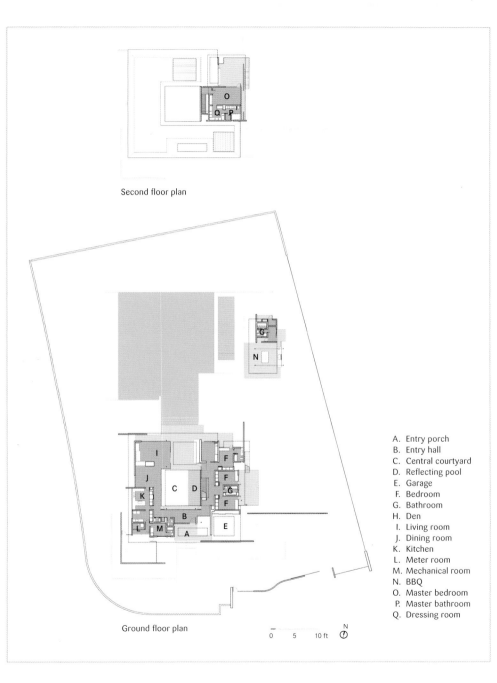

Second floor plan

Some peripheral walls are extended to direct the views and to protect the house from the winds and exposure to streets. The roofs also extend to form deep eaves that protect the windows from the sun and to cover the terraces, while accentuating the horizontality of the house.

A. Entry porch
B. Entry hall
C. Central courtyard
D. Reflecting pool
E. Garage
F. Bedroom
G. Bathroom
H. Den
I. Living room
J. Dining room
K. Kitchen
L. Meter room
M. Mechanical room
N. BBQ
O. Master bedroom
P. Master bathroom
Q. Dressing room

Ground floor plan

0   5   10 ft

N

097

The courtyard house provides additional outdoor space, improves circulation, and creates drama.

The interior public areas are conceived as flexible spaces that can be totally enclosed or open to the central patio. When open, the central patio facilitates the circulation between the different spaces arranged around it and promotes interaction among their occupants.

098

Courtyard houses follow traditional home construction, where the main rooms are arranged around a patio. Courtyard houses are becoming increasingly popular, as they provide spatial solutions to housing in dense inner cities.

099

The use of wood in wall paneling, floors and doors achieves a cohesive and elegant interior décor. The rich color and grain of the wood contrast with a minimalistic color palette, adding warmth and texture.

Retrospect Vineyards, a twenty-acre plot in the Russian River Valley, has been producing pinot noir grapes and selling them to nearby wineries for fifteen years. When the new owners bought the property, they knew they wanted to have a greater involvement in the winemaking process. The result was a modern home designed to function as a family retreat and a working vineyard, respecting the privacy of the residents without hampering the functionality of the land.

Retrospect Vineyards

Swatt | Miers Architects

Windsor, California,
United States

© Marion Brenner,
Russell Abraham

This new home has been designed to provide casual indoor-outdoor living spaces that take full advantage of the magnificent wine country site.

100

A design incorporating the environmental conditions, the principles of a design, and the requirements set by a client organizes the built work and the natural landscape into a functional and environmentally friendly project.

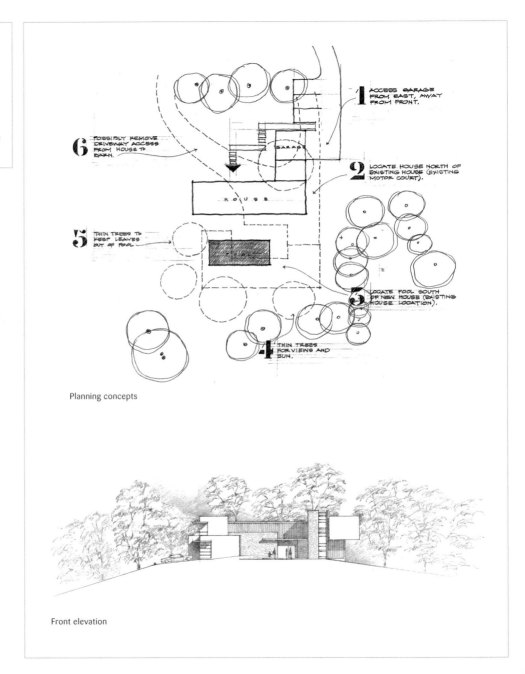

1 ACCESS GARAGE FROM EAST, AWAY FROM FRONT.

6 POSSIBLY REMOVE DRIVEWAY ACCESS FROM HOUSE TO BARN.

2 LOCATE HOUSE NORTH OF EXISTING HOUSE (EXISTING MOTOR COURT).

5 THIN TREES TO KEEP LEAVES OUT OF POOL

3 LOCATE POOL SOUTH OF NEW HOUSE (EXISTING HOUSE LOCATION).

4 THIN TREES FOR VIEWS AND SUN.

Planning concepts

Front elevation

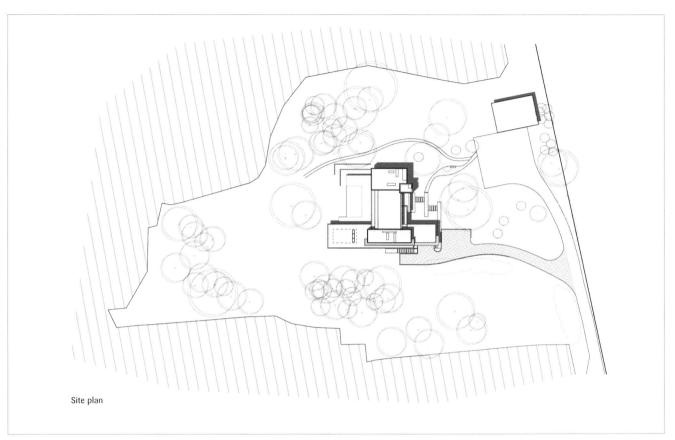

Site plan

101

The process that begins with an analysis of the existing conditions results in a final plan that includes all the necessary details to achieve an optimal symbiosis between the environmental conditions and the built work.

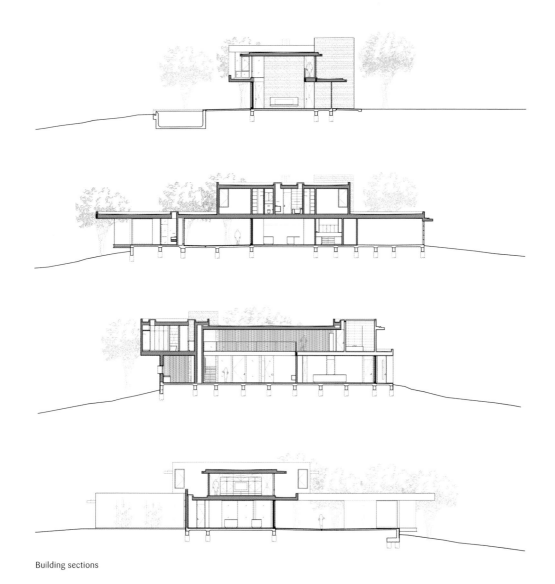

Building sections

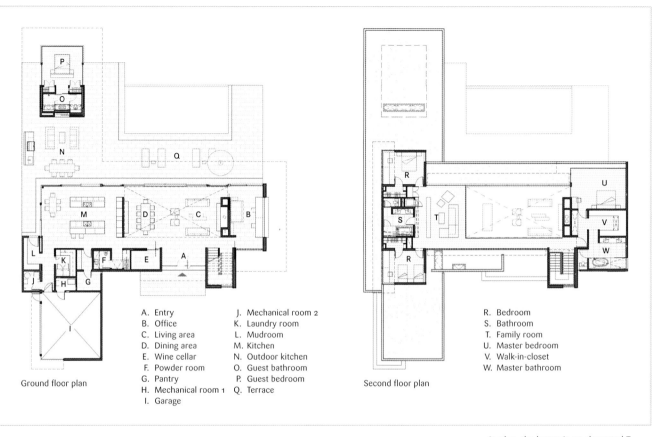

A. Entry
B. Office
C. Living area
D. Dining area
E. Wine cellar
F. Powder room
G. Pantry
H. Mechanical room 1
I. Garage
J. Mechanical room 2
K. Laundry room
L. Mudroom
M. Kitchen
N. Outdoor kitchen
O. Guest bathroom
P. Guest bedroom
Q. Terrace

R. Bedroom
S. Bathroom
T. Family room
U. Master bedroom
V. Walk-in-closet
W. Master bathroom

Ground floor plan

Second floor plan

In plan, the house is an elongated T, which creates a relatively opaque and private entry courtyard on the north side. In contrast, the south side of the house is all glass, including large sliding glass doors that open the interior spaces to an expansive swimming pool terrace, overlooking the vineyards below.

102

Glass enclosures enhance the geometry formed by the solid parts of a building, generally creating a floating effect.

A deep, floating roof spans over the main house and a glass guesthouse, creating a sun-protected outdoor kitchen and dining terrace with dramatic pool and vineyard views on two sides.

103

Large structural spans on exterior walls allow big openings maximizing the connection between interior and exterior.

104

Windows can be sized and placed to control the amount of light that reaches an interior space. Orientation and sun's path are factors to take into account.

105

Rooms that have glass walls
on more than two sides are
fully exposed to the exterior.
The glass is a protective layer,
but the feeling is that of being
outside, experiencing the
environment, the changing
seasons, and the light.

106

Windows catch the low sun angles in the winter and limit the high-angled rays in the summer, while skylights often do the opposite.

The Shoshone Residence is site-responsive with simple forms that blend with the landscape of flat, grassy sites with spectacular views of distant high mountains. The 4,500-square-foot home boasts generous, yet intimate spaces that take full advantage of one hundred and twenty acres of open space to the south and the dramatic mountains to the north and south. The design approach of the house is aimed at maximizing family interaction and encouraging outdoor living. This is translated into a U-shape configuration framing a courtyard that acts as the central gathering space of the home.

Shoshone Residence

Carney Logan Burke Architects

Wilson, Wyoming, United States

© Audrey Hall

107

Courtyard ideas generally take cue from the buildings they complement. Hardscapes, formed by paved areas and retaining walls, promote a harmonious transition between a building and the surrounding landscape.

Deep overhangs protect the building from harsh weather. The exterior is clad in cedar siding, which dissolves into screens, creating pattern and depth at the building entry points.

108

Site analysis is perhaps
the most important step to
develop a successful house
project. Generally, it involves
climate, orientation, soils,
slope, vegetation, hydrology,
and shadow pattern studies.

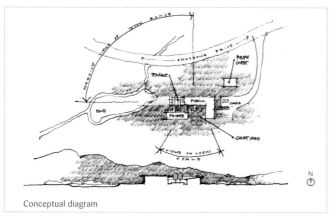

Conceptual diagram

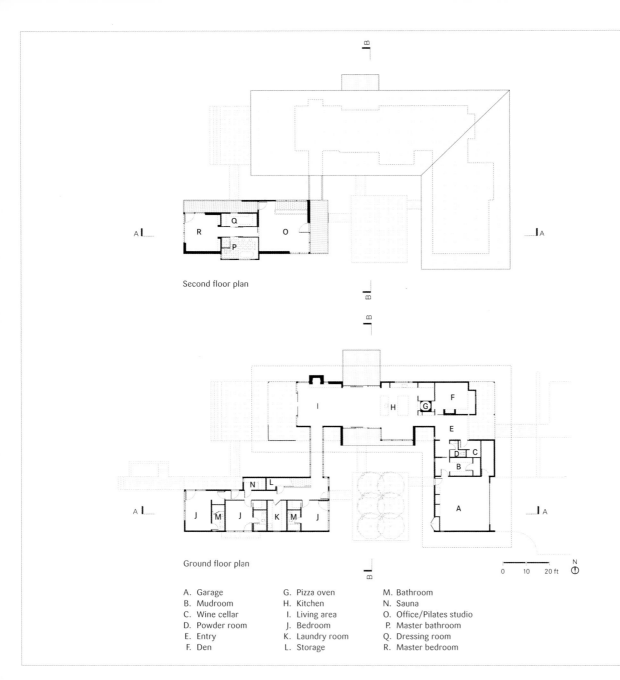

Second floor plan

Ground floor plan

A. Garage
B. Mudroom
C. Wine cellar
D. Powder room
E. Entry
F. Den

G. Pizza oven
H. Kitchen
I. Living area
J. Bedroom
K. Laundry room
L. Storage

M. Bathroom
N. Sauna
O. Office/Pilates studio
P. Master bathroom
Q. Dressing room
R. Master bedroom

0   10   20 ft
N

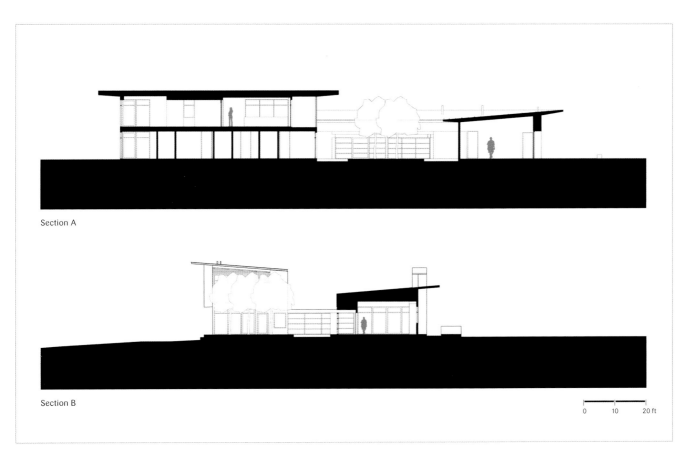

Section A

Section B

0   10   20 ft

109

The climate, the environment, the building regulations, and the overall building aesthetics guide the resulting shape of a roof. For instance, the slope of a roof is generally proportional to the snow load or rainfall.

110

An entry porch creates a cohesive transition between the exterior and the interior. It creates a sense of arrival and offers a prelude to the rest of the house.

111

Sliding doors are easy to use and do not take up valuable floor area, as opposed to French doors, which do need space to swing open and close.

112

Provide every room in your house with plenty of easily accessible storage. When it comes to home value, abundant storage space is a quality that home owners greatly appreciate.

The spectacular site and views, as well as the modest program, led to the organization of the main house and guest quarters in separate buildings configured to form outdoor spaces. With mountains rising to the northwest and a stream cutting through the southeast corner of the lot, the placement of the main house and guest cabin responds to the two scales of the site.

The two wings of the main house define the exterior space to the northwest, which is visually connected to the mountains beyond. At a more intimate scale, the garden walls of the main house and guest cabin enclose the entry court to the southeast.

John Dodge Residence

Dynia Architects

Teton County, Wyoming, United States

© Dynia Architects

113

Lighting design enhances the architectural appeal of a building in addition to fulfilling functional needs, such as making the building visible and illuminating paths that lead to the house's entry at night.

North elevation

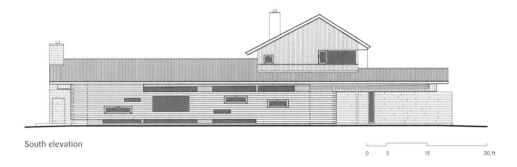

South elevation

0	5	15	30 ft

114

The placement of windows establishes a visual dialogue between the interior and the exterior, framing views, while at the same time being an important design aspect of a building's façades.

115

Clear circulation paths contribute to the definition of spaces and to the way we experience them. The approach to these circulation paths can vary from a few steps through a small space to a long processional path.

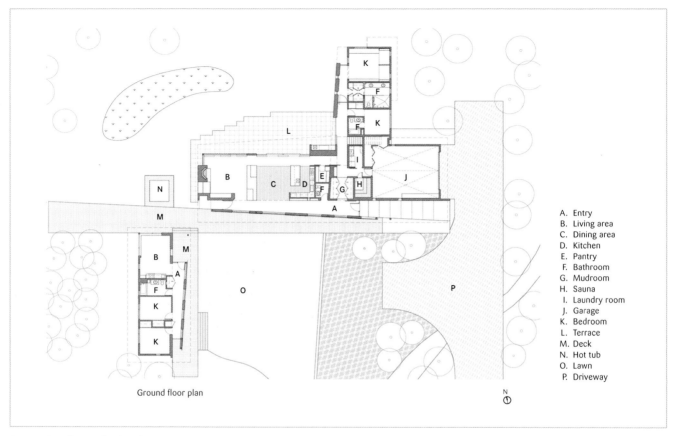

Ground floor plan

A. Entry
B. Living area
C. Dining area
D. Kitchen
E. Pantry
F. Bathroom
G. Mudroom
H. Sauna
I. Laundry room
J. Garage
K. Bedroom
L. Terrace
M. Deck
N. Hot tub
O. Lawn
P. Driveway

N

A concrete wall, extending into the landscape, defines the major circulation spine. Public spaces open off this spine toward the views to the mountains. Secondary spaces branch off to the north and south, forming the private wing of the main house and the guest cabin respectively.

With regulations restricting the roof forms, the structural trusses are shaped to lift the ceiling planes toward light and the views of the landscape. Primary interior spaces open to the landscape, connecting interior and exterior spaces.

Port Ludlow Residence is a compact, 2,400-square-foot modern house on a wooded waterfront property, facing the Hood Canal in Washington State. The house has a number of sustainable building features, including two-by-eight wall construction, providing forty percent greater insulation value; generous glass surfaces to provide natural lighting and ventilation; large overhangs for sun and rain protection; metal siding—recycled steel—for maximum durability, and a heat pump mechanical system for maximum energy efficiency.

Port Ludlow Residence

FINNE Architects

Port Ludlow, Washington, United States

© Benjamin Benschneider

The main living volume is completely glazed, with twelve-foot-high glass walls facing the view, and large eight-foot-square sliding glass doors that open to a slightly raised wood deck, creating a seamless indoor-outdoor space.

The house has a compact floor plan composed of two parts: a large glassed-in living area that faces the Hood Canal to the east, and a two-story living block, containing service areas and bedrooms.

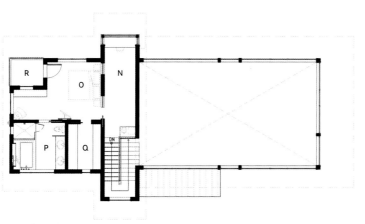

Second floor plan

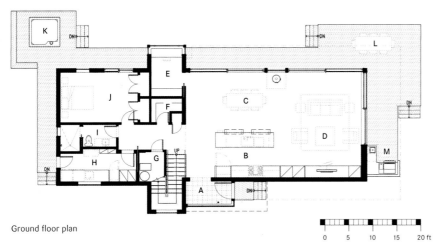

Ground floor plan

A. Entry
B. Kitchen
C. Dining area
D. Living area
E. Office
F. Pantry
G. Mechanical room
H. Laundry room
I. Bathroom
J. Guestroom
K. Hot tub
L. Outdoor dining area
M. Outdoor kitchen
N. Study
O. Master bedroom
P. Master bathroom
Q. Walk-in-closet
R. Balcony

0   5   10   15   20 ft

116

A passive solar design allows a building to take in abundant natural light through large glass surfaces, while protecting the interior from the elements by means of deep overhangs.

Interior finishes are simple and elegant, with IPE wood flooring, zebrawood cabinet doors with mahogany end panels, quartz and limestone countertops, and Douglas fir trim and doors.

In the spirit of sustainable architecture, the house incorporates materials such as locally-sourced Douglas fir, engineered quartz, natural wool carpet, LED lighting, linoleum floors, and low-VOC paints.

The Sands Point House is site sensitive both in regard to of its natural environment and the building tradition of the area. It consists of a renovated nineteenth-century farmhouse and a new timber and glass addition cantilevering above existing stone walls. The design explores structural and spatial principles and features building details that are as visually appealing as they are functionally effective. To complete the design, a terraced garden wraps around the addition, connecting upper and lower outdoor areas.

Sands Point House

Ole Sondresen Architect

Sands Point, New York, United States

© Edward Caruso

A Douglas fir post and Glulam beam structure supports the shed roof of the new addition. The roof is angled to open up the main living spaces to the pool and the terraced landscape.

Section through hot tub

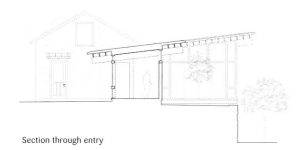

Section through entry

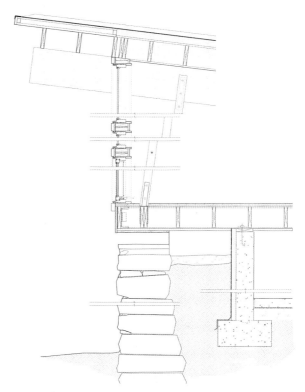

Wall section detail

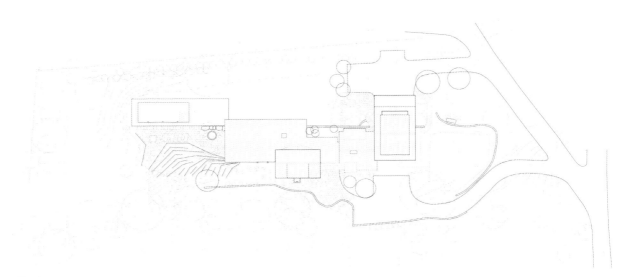

Site plan

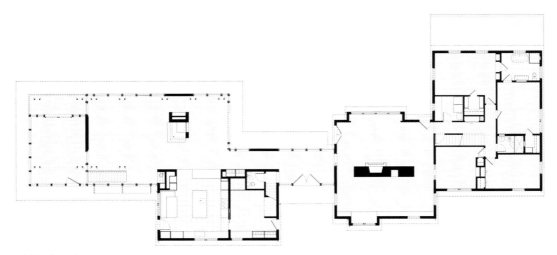

Addition floor plan

117

The dialogue between old and new construction can be approached in two different ways: one that fuses both to create a uniform look, or one that creates a clear distinction between the two, for instance, by using contrasting materials.

118

A custom-made fireplace generally draws attention and serves as a focal point in a home. It can create contrast and accentuate the height of a room. When it occupies a central position, it acts as organizer of the space.

The fireplace in the timber and glass addition is one of the various elements that make the design of this home so special. The board-formed concrete fireplace separates the living and dining areas.

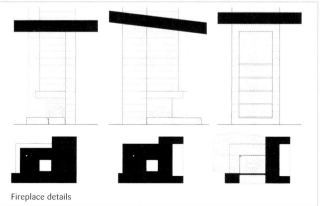

Fireplace details

119

Smart modern bathrooms can combine modern plumbing fixtures and rustic elements to create a functional, but comfortable and cozy atmosphere.

The primary idea driving the design of this spectacular house was to create a living space with a single roof floating over it. Its configuration and orientation adapts to the slope of the site following a northwest to southeast direction, which enjoys breathtaking ocean views to the east and to the south. It was important that the design maximized the connection to these views. One enters at the upper level of the double volume looking toward the ocean. The concept behind the landscaping was to reinstate the shrubland and let the building float over this restored surface.

Cove 3 House

SAOTA and Antoni Associates

Knysna, South Africa

© SAOTA, John Devonport & Micky Hoyle courtesy of VISI

120

Cove 3 House is a good example of how a glass pavilion can be in harmony with nature. At daytime, the glazed walls mirror its surroundings. At night, the house glows and its walls seem to disappear to fuse interior and exterior.

The roof is set at a sufficiently high level that it is out of one's line of sight from the living space. This creates the illusion that one is sitting in the landscape rather than in a room looking out into a landscape.

The building is approached from the northwest at the top of the site, where the elevation is low and horizontal. The choice of materials such as off-shutter concrete, Rheinzink roofing, timber cladding, stone, and exposed aggregate will allow the building to fade into the landscape as it ages.

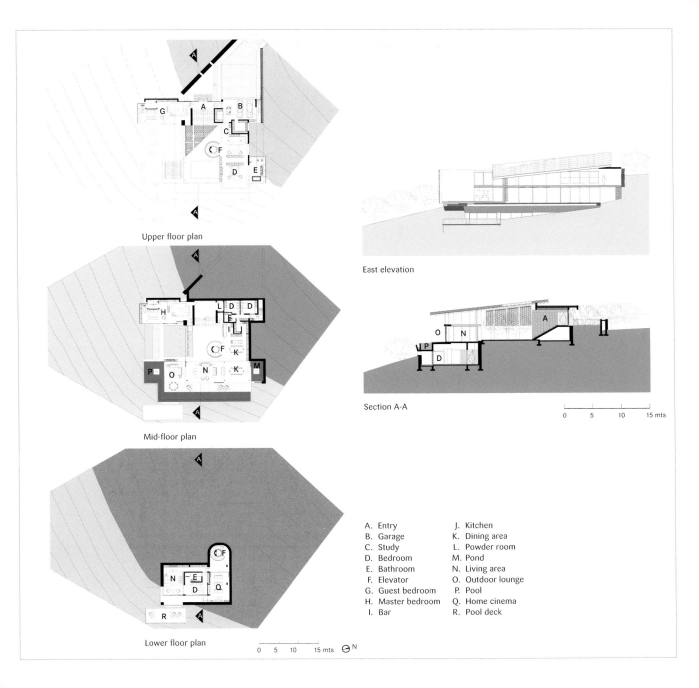

Upper floor plan

East elevation

Mid-floor plan

Section A-A

0 5 10 15 mts

Lower floor plan

0 5 10 15 mts

N

A. Entry
B. Garage
C. Study
D. Bedroom
E. Bathroom
F. Elevator
G. Guest bedroom
H. Master bedroom
I. Bar
J. Kitchen
K. Dining area
L. Powder room
M. Pond
N. Living area
O. Outdoor lounge
P. Pool
Q. Home cinema
R. Pool deck

121

To enhance the sculptural character of a staircase, it is critical that it is surrounded by a generous open space, so one can understand how it relates to the space in which it is contained.

The bedrooms have curved curtain tracks that create very intimate sleeping spaces at night, which contrast with the very open daytime character.

122

Make the most of an idyllic setting to create a bathroom that is not a plain, utilitarian room, but rather a place for relaxation. What better way to promote a sense of well-being than to surround yourself with the beauty of nature?

Nestled into the edge of a hilltop, this home offers panoramic views of South Austin. The building, which is vertically stratified across a split-level configuration, allows for a wide variety of spatial experiences and view opportunities as one ascends the central stair tower. The design reinforces this vertical procession, starting with a concrete plinth that retains earth at the sunken garage and becomes the foundation, the exposed steel beams, which support the heavy loads of the second story and roof deck, and the cantilevered Glulam beams at the high roof, orienting this level to its primary downtown view.

Barton Hills Residence

A Parallel Architecture

Austin, Texas, United States

© Topher Ayrhart

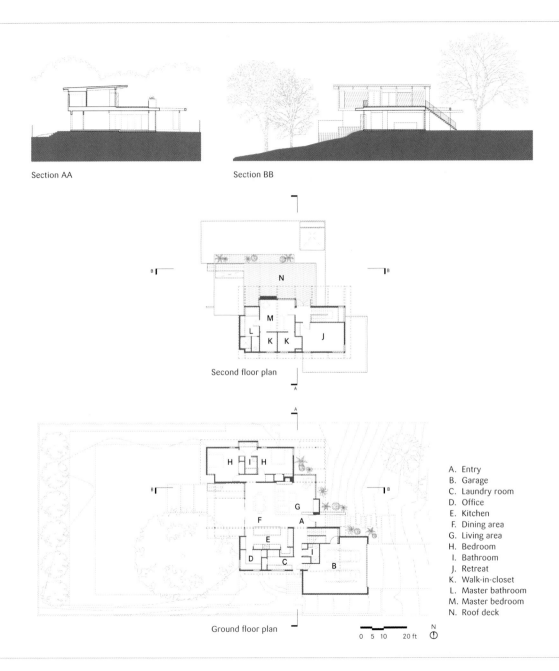

Section AA

Section BB

Second floor plan

Ground floor plan

A. Entry
B. Garage
C. Laundry room
D. Office
E. Kitchen
F. Dining area
G. Living area
H. Bedroom
I. Bathroom
J. Retreat
K. Walk-in-closet
L. Master bathroom
M. Master bedroom
N. Roof deck

N

0 5 10   20 ft

123

Exterior spaces make the design of a house complete, responding to aesthetic and functional requirements. They also contribute to a careful integration of architecture with its immediate—and distant—surroundings.

Windows can be a defining feature of a home. Floor-to-ceiling windows have a contemporary design quality that can be accentuated by details such as the thickness and material of mullions.

125

Floor-to-ceiling windows look great, but they also create room-furnishing challenges. Choose your furniture according to the amount of wall surface, and complete the décor with freestanding furniture.

In rural areas, with no houses in the vicinity, privacy becomes a minor concern. This is the chance to open up the house to the outdoors with open spaces and large windows in every room, including the bathroom.

This house is nestled into a steep hill with mature cedar and Douglas fir to the west and ocean views to the south. Due to its proximity to a sloping creek-side bank to the west, the house was subject to strict environmental and geotechnical conditions, including a required setback from the top of the bank that pushed the building's foundation eastwards. The resultant footprint was awkwardly narrow, so to gain back valuable space, a portion of the main and upper floor cantilevers out past the foundation, allowing the native creek-side vegetation to grow up and under the new structure.

Russet Residence

Splyce Design

West Vancouver,
British Columbia, Canada

© Ivan Hunter

The overall porosity and openness
of the house reveals a deliberate
orchestration of circulation and views,
while a balance of solidity and robust
materiality and massing serves to
anchor the house to the land.

The front of the house is modest in
scale, set off by a large mature cedar
that anchors the front yard. The
topography of the site reveals itself
as one descends an exterior staircase
adjacent to the forest and follows
an exposed concrete wall to the
main entry.

Lower floor plan

Main floor plan

Upper floor plan

A. Wine cellar	H. Terrace	O. Powder room	V. Garage
B. Media room	I. Fire pit	P. Dining room	W. Master bathroom
C. Bedroom	J. Deck	Q. Living area	X. Walk-in-closet
D. Bathroom	K. Pool	R. Kitchen	Y. Master bedroom
E. Rec room	L. Hot tub	S. Laundry room	Z. Mudroom
F. Storage	M. Entry	T. Playroom	
G. Outdoor kitchen	N. Office	U. Mechanical room	

127

Building a stepped house on a sloped site allows each level to enjoy exterior spaces and views. The stepped structure can be reflected on the interior with a layout that focuses as much on circulation as on room layout.

The reclamation of space is clearly pronounced in the dining room, where it projects fifteen feet out past the concrete foundation wall. By extending the glazing panels on all three sides of the room, the space dissolves into the adjacent forest canopy.

From the staircase that connects all
three floors, one gains an understanding
and orientation of the home in
relation to the site, its topography,
and movement of the sun across the
building by way of the wall-to-wall
skylight above.

Subtle hints of views to the sky, ocean, and forest are suggested from the staircases, but it's not until one moves deeper into the house that they are fully revealed.

128

Concrete flooring is a resistant, stylish choice for a kitchen as well as for other spaces. As kitchens often blend with dining and living areas as part of a large space, the floor can unify these different areas, creating a cohesive design.

129

Different flooring materials and different floor heights are design solutions that can be used to separate functions sharing the same space, while maintaining visual connection.

130

The continuity of an interior space can be preserved by keeping its perimeter free of obstacles and introducing interior partitions that are short of the ceiling.

131

A strategically placed mirror, properly sized for a particular room, can alter the perception of the space and improve its look by reflecting views and magnifying light.

The bending volumes of this house echo the shifting character of its coastal sandy site. It was important that the house fit into its fragile location. In response to this requirement, the house—composed of two blocks—gently brushes the terrain in some parts, and is completely elevated off the ground in others.

The main house is an assembly of cantilevered planes and volumes that culminate in a large living/dining space defined by an arcing roof. Separated from the main house by a screen porch and a contiguous deck is an art/thinking studio that floats fourteen feet above the ground.

House of Shifting Sands

Ruhl Walker Architects

Cape Cod, Massachusetts, United States

© Jane Messinger

The house is sited gently on the lower slope of a dramatic sixty-foot-high coastal bank. Surrounded by scrub pines and miles of undeveloped beaches, it is oriented to maximize views and summer breezes, while minimizing its exposure to winter storms.

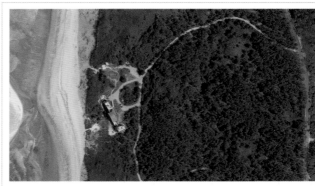

Aerial view of site

The main house touches down gently, halfway up the coastal bank so that the natural landscape retains its primacy.

A breezeway, splitting the ground floor of the house into two sections, extends to the sky through a hole in the main living level. This hole acts as a thermal chimney to enhance natural ventilation.

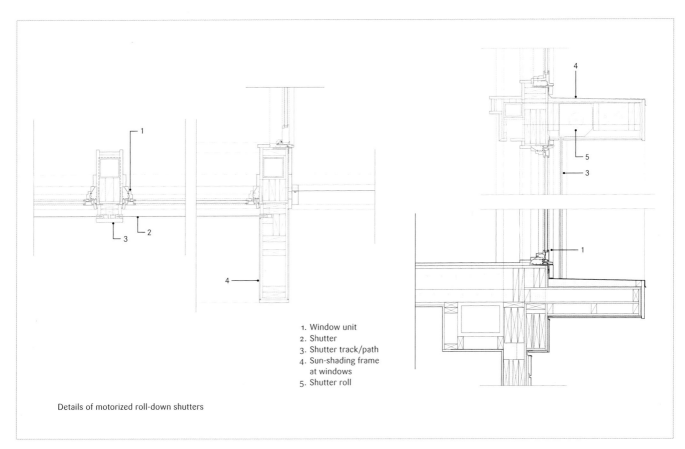

1. Window unit
2. Shutter
3. Shutter track/path
4. Sun-shading frame
   at windows
5. Shutter roll

Details of motorized roll-down shutters

132

The motorized roll-down
shutters provide the added
benefit of being an outer
protective layer, preventing
debris from ever reaching the
glass surface. This adds to the
longevity of windows.

Each of the house's volumes is cantilevered beyond the structure below, to enhance the floating and shifting effect that is further reinforced with lighting.

Rendered section facing Cape Cod Bay

Rendered section facing north

Rendered section facing south

Building section. Views from seating position

Building section. Views from standing position

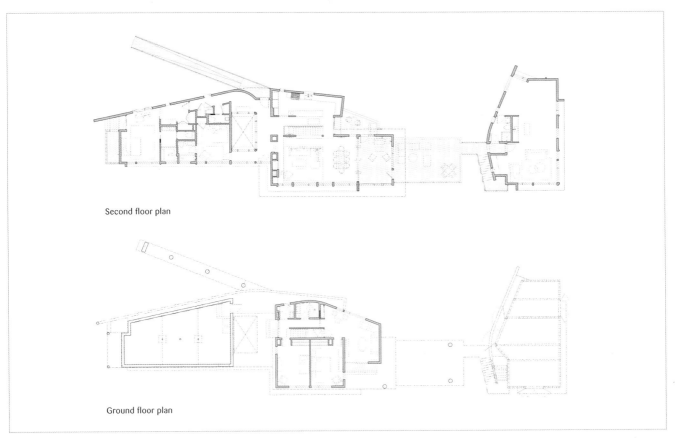

Second floor plan

Ground floor plan

The house's form curves and shifts
softly with the natural topography.
Over time the new native and drought-
resistant landscaping will grow back
tight to the house as if both had always
been there together.

The main living spaces are gathered
together under an asymmetrically arcing
cedar and copper roof. A wall of hidden
cabinetry and a fireplace are special
features of the living spaces, which
are kept simple so as not to compete
with the glass wall and the priceless
views beyond.

133

The orientation of a kitchen is a design aspect that needs to be considered early in the design phase. Orienting it to the south or southwest will require some sort of shading in the summer, such as blinds, awnings, or overhangs.

This spectacular house sits on a beautiful 3.8-acre, gently sloping parcel, with mature oak, cedar, and pine trees. Requirements for the design included open planning for interior spaces, zoning of the functions to provide a clear separation between public and private spaces, and maximizing views, as well as a strong, symbiotic relationship between building and landscape. The result is an L-shape configuration that enjoys abundant natural light thanks to the generous use of glass and high ceilings, and dramatic short and long views.

Vidalakis Residence

Swatt | Miers Architects

Portola Valley, California,
United States

© Russel Abraham

The architectural language is simple. Built of natural materials—primarily cast-in-place concrete and wood—this new modern home is assertive in its formal expression as it simultaneously reaches out to, and embraces, the natural landscape.

Perpendicular to the house and the topography, a seventy-five-foot-long swimming pool, wood deck, and lawn area define the western edge of the immediate landscape with precise geometry.

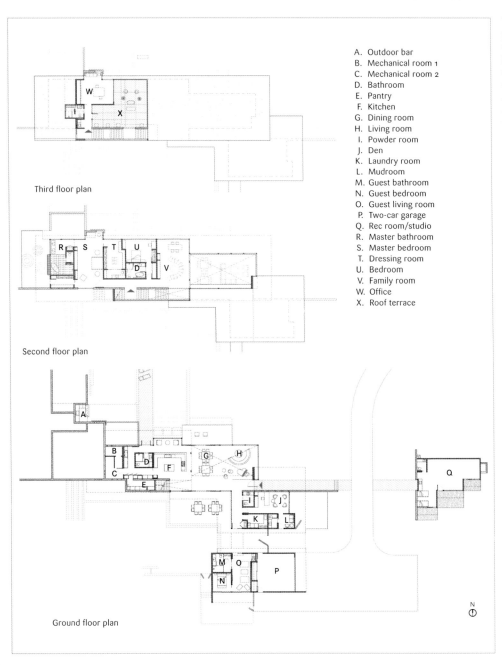

Third floor plan

Second floor plan

Ground floor plan

A. Outdoor bar
B. Mechanical room 1
C. Mechanical room 2
D. Bathroom
E. Pantry
F. Kitchen
G. Dining room
H. Living room
I. Powder room
J. Den
K. Laundry room
L. Mudroom
M. Guest bathroom
N. Guest bedroom
O. Guest living room
P. Two-car garage
Q. Rec room/studio
R. Master bathroom
S. Master bedroom
T. Dressing room
U. Bedroom
V. Family room
W. Office
X. Roof terrace

The design is based on an L-shaped plan with a linear concrete wall defining circulation and extending into the landscape to form the edges of the entry and the family courtyard. The plan organization creates two major outdoor areas: a private landscaped courtyard on the south side, and a more public terrace for entertaining on the north.

N

134

Transparent elevations offer a strong connection between the interior of a house and its surrounding outdoor spaces. Transparency can also allow for interior elements such as staircases to be expressed on the exterior.

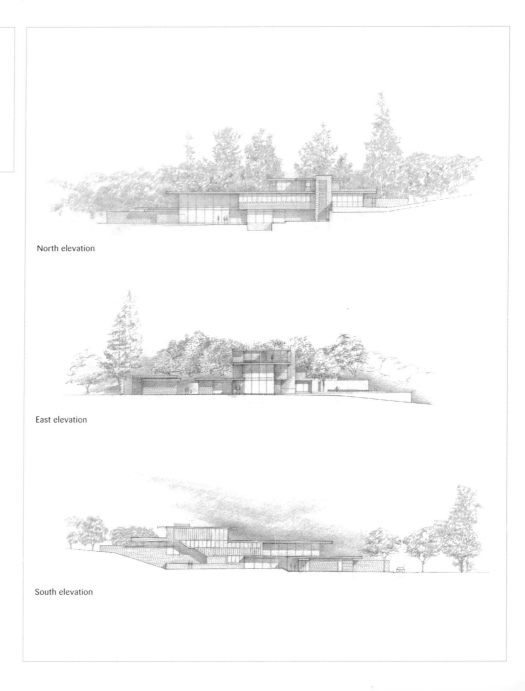

North elevation

East elevation

South elevation

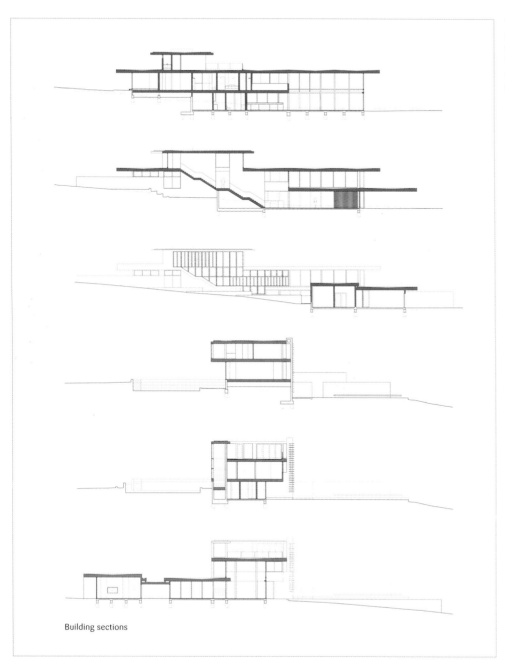

The slope of the terrain led to a design that uses the principles of terracing, resulting in a stepped style structure. This helped in breaking down the scale of the building and minimizing the visual impact on the landscape.

Building sections

135

Glass walls lend transparency to a home, allowing the landscape to be the backdrop to a room. A dramatic double height enhances this experience, raising the ceiling height well above sightline.

The spaces are organized along
a circulation spine that includes a
spectacular mahogany staircase against
the glass wall with views of the south
courtyard.

136

An indoor-outdoor bathroom can be the ultimate luxurious retreat with floor-to-ceiling sliding glass doors and abundant greenery serving as screen for privacy.

137

Turn your bathroom into a luxurious personal world with rich woods and semi-precious stone accented with warm, soothing lighting to re-create the spa experience at home.

The house is organized as a series of volumes, arranged linearly and positioned to optimize views of an undulating landscape and nearby forest. The structure itself becomes a threshold and defines a more intimate, manicured outdoor environment between the house and the edge of the forest.

The rigorous, refined, and geometric forms of the house are designed in sharp contrast to the natural landscape. Not only is this contrast intended to magnify the beauty of the site, but it also enables the house to provide a framework for experiencing an inherently beautiful landscape.

4 Springs Lane

Robert M. Gurney, Architect

Rappahannock County, Virginia, United States

© Maxwell MacKenzie Architectural Photographer

The design of the house is simultaneously complex and distilled, largely due to the combination of materials—glass, wood, stone, and fiber cement panels—that render a more complex composition, while garnering a serene unity.

A two-story living area has floor-to-ceiling windows at each end, providing a lens through which to view the distant landscape.

138

Good outdoor lighting adds to safety at night to reach an entry. It also contributes greatly to the visual appeal of a front garden.

The linear organization allows the majority of spaces to maintain the views, while providing accessibility to a terrace with a swimming pool and the manicured landscape.

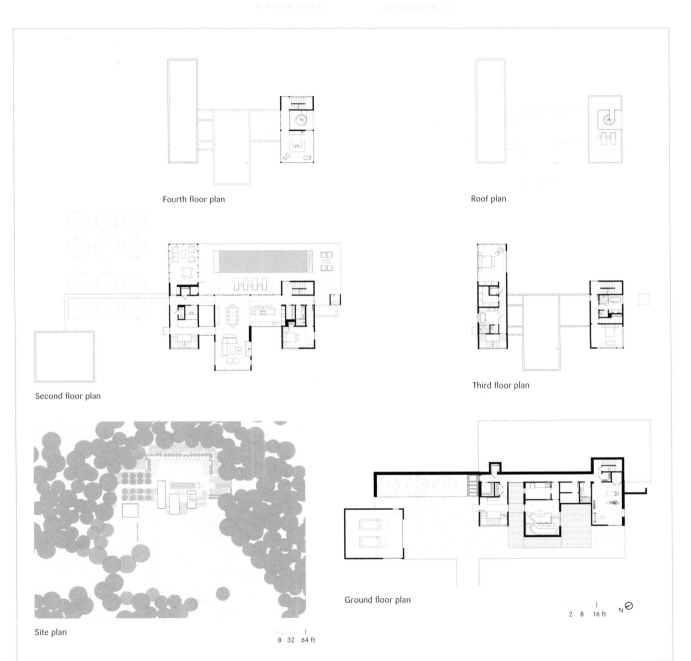

Fourth floor plan

Roof plan

Second floor plan

Third floor plan

Site plan

Ground floor plan

8 32 64 ft

2 8 16 ft   N

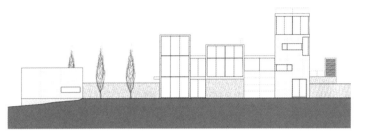

North elevation

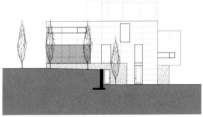

East elevation

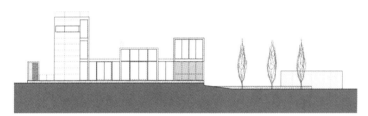

South elevation

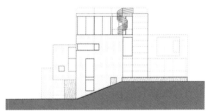

West elevation

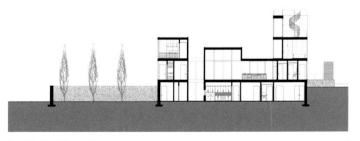

East-West building section

2 8   16 ft

139

Proportion, texture, and light are design elements that can be used to organize and animate a project.

Interior spaces are active and intricate, tranquil and minimal. With vistas in all directions, large expanses of glass allow the landscape views to provide the primary sensory experience.

140

Glass walls offer the advantage of diffusing the separation between interior and exterior, allowing the surrounding natural environment to be part of the built space.

141

Long views and beautiful landscape can be an inspiring environment to a workspace. With nothing more than a few basic furnishings, the beautiful scenery sets the perfect serene atmosphere for concentration.

A steep sixteen-acre property in a densely wooded area is the backdrop to this house. The initial design strategy focused on manipulating the site to preserve as much of its natural topography as possible. As a result, a two-hundred-foot-long board-formed concrete retaining wall runs north-south along the site's east edge, exposing new plateaus for buildings, garden, and meadow. Clinging to this wall, the guesthouse anchors the building assembly in the steep hillside, while the main house and deck project out from the landform into the treetops.

Red Rock House

Anmahian Winton Architects

Red Rock, New York,
United States

© Jane Messinger Photography

A minimal material palette evokes both rusticity and precision, reflecting the juxtaposed orders of landscape and architecture. Buildings are clad in a high-performance rain screen of knotty western red cedar, milled with multiple profiles to generate a pattern that changes with the sun's movement.

Upper floor plan

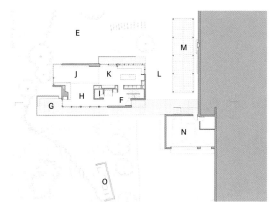

Main floor plan

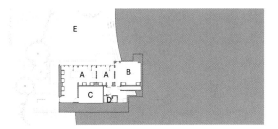

Lower floor plan

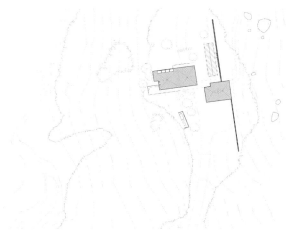

Site plan

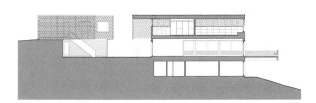

Building section

A. Art studio
B. Fitness studio
C. Mechanical room
D. Bathroom
E. North meadow
F. Entry
G. Bluestone balcony
H. Den
I. Powder room
J. Living room
K. Kitchen/dining area

L. East garden
M. Garden trellis
N. Garage
O. Mechanical area
P. Master bathroom
Q. Study
R. Changing room
S. Master bedroom
T. Guest living
U. Guest bedroom

N

142

White interiors can draw
attention to a contemporary
vocabulary and minimal
form that underscore the
relationship between built
work and natural landscape
and emphasize the play of
light on the different surfaces.

An existing A-frame house was too small and its orientation did not take advantage of the beautiful setting. Nonetheless, the new owners saw that the site had potential, but most important, they saw in it a pleasant place to accommodate a family with growing kids in a lush green area with the convenient proximity to a town. In order to maximize views and solar access, the house is composed of two rectangular volumes. A massive concrete lower floor anchors the house to the hillside, while a wood and glass upper floor with cantilevering decks allows visual connection with the surrounding landscape.

Invermay House

Moloney Architects

Ballarat, Victoria, Australia
© Michael Kai

The exterior materials were chosen
to echo the colors of the surrounding
landscape. The material selection
—which includes spotted-gum cladding
and blackbutt for the window frames
and batten shade screens—was
influenced by the location of the
house in a bushfire-prone area.

North elevation

East elevation

South elevation

West elevation

The house is composed of a series of intersecting parts that combine solid forms and voids. This design approach achieves contrasts between heavy and light forms, as well as opaque and transparent surfaces.

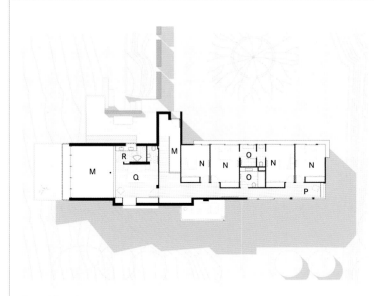

A. Entry
B. Dining room
C. Recreation room
D. Garage
E. Powder room
F. Laundry room
G. Study
H. Pantry
I. Kitchen
J. Breakfast nook
K. Living room
L. Deck
M. Double-height space
N. Bedroom
O. Bathroom
P. Reading nook
Q. Master bedroom
R. Master bathroom

Second floor plan

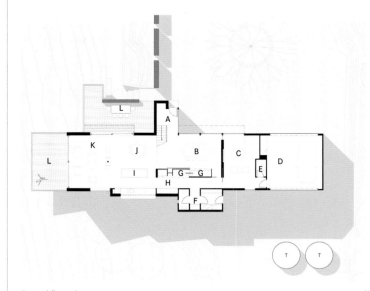

Ground floor plan

143

Think outside the box to make the most of available space, transforming underused closet space into a functional home office.

144

Steel woodstoves are an
energy-efficient alternative
to traditional fireplaces and
allow the opportunity to
express an original design.

145

Integrated kitchen designs
offer a modern and clean
look. In open-plan layouts,
the selected finish can tie
the kitchen with adjacent
areas, such as the living
and dining room.

The mirror-open shelf extends in front of the window. More that adding to the storage capacity of the bathroom, this design gesture is mainly aesthetic. Its proportions echo that of the vanity and the section in front of the window minimally obstructs the view.

The design of this house is deeply connected to the landscape, relying on interpretations of specific vernacular principles such as tropical modernism, and building styles like the Dogtrot and the American glass pavilion. The design gives architectural primacy to composition, and materiality to the logics of construction. Its location near a river and the dense vegetation in the area guided the design. As a result, the house floats five feet off the ground in response to the building codes, in anticipation of rising-water threats and the will to be "light on the land."

Brillhart House

Brillhart Architecture

Miami, Florida, United States

© Stefani Fachini, Bruce Buck, Jake Brillhart

The 1,500-square-foot house features fifty feet of uninterrupted glass spanning the full length of both the front and back sides of the house. Shutters along the front façade provide privacy and protection against the elements, while creating an outdoor room with ever-changing light and shadow patterns.

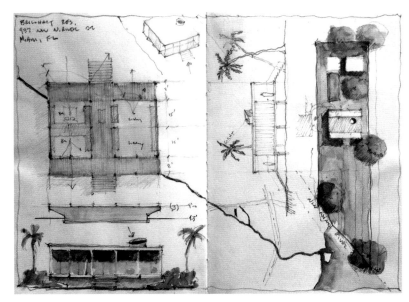

Design development sketches

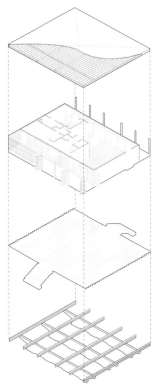

Exploded axonometric

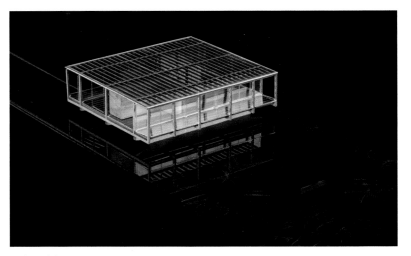

Study model

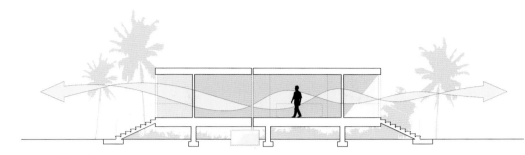

Cross-ventilation diagram

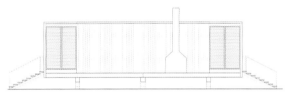

Side elevation

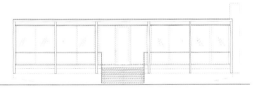

Front elevation. Open shutters

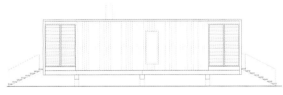

Side elevation

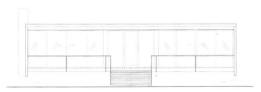

Back elevation

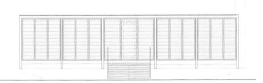

Front elevation. Shutters closed

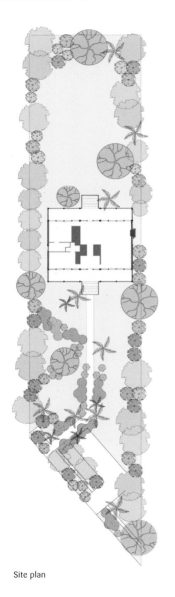

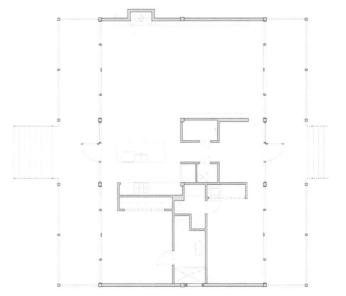

Building section

Site plan

Floor plan

146

Function and comfort are the goals to be pursued in the design of a space, followed by aesthetics and unity obtained through furnishings that blend and harmonize with the architecture of the room that contains them.

The interior and the exterior spaces are also melded seamlessly together. Four sets of sliding glass doors allow the house to be entirely open when desired.

147

A light color palette and a simple selection of finishes and furnishings can infuse a room with a sense of well-being, balance, and harmony.

148

The color variations of wood and its grain give character to a room. In a bathroom, wood can be combined with other finishes such as stone and ceramic tile, or can be used against a contrasting finish like a light paint color.

This unique home combines country living with urban lifestyle. Its striking composition made of three long cantilevering structures on top of a secluded hill gives the spaces of the house commanding views into the woods and the feeling of being suspended in the trees. Entirely clad in cedar, the house boasts a warm texture that will tarnish over time to facilitate the integration of the building into the natural surroundings.

Cabin in the Woods

Rangr Studio

Southampton, New York, United States

© Paul Warchol

The upper floor cantilever was achieved with an all-wood structure, using engineered lumber to create beams out of the full height of the side walls.

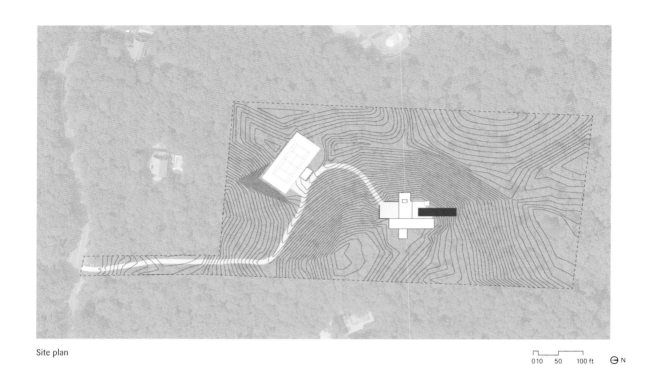

Site plan

010 50   100 ft   ⊖ N

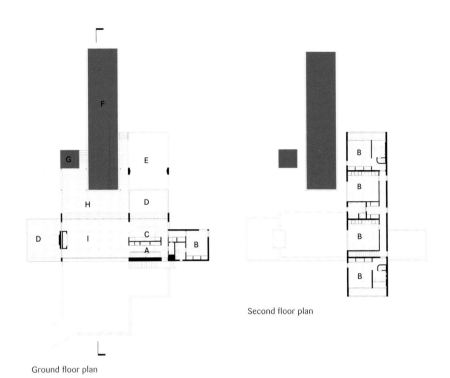

Ground floor plan

Second floor plan

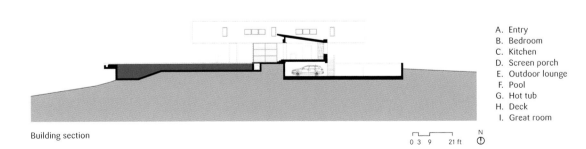

Building section

A. Entry
B. Bedroom
C. Kitchen
D. Screen porch
E. Outdoor lounge
F. Pool
G. Hot tub
H. Deck
I. Great room

0 3 9   21 ft

N

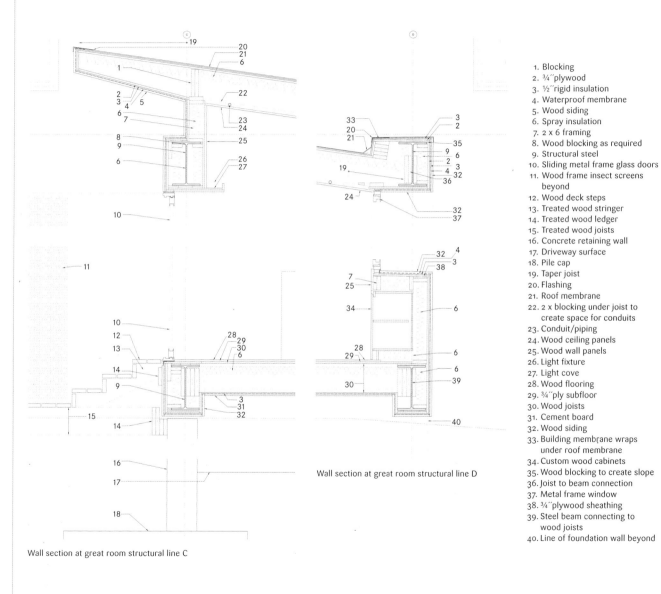

1. Blocking
2. ¾″ plywood
3. ½″ rigid insulation
4. Waterproof membrane
5. Wood siding
6. Spray insulation
7. 2 x 6 framing
8. Wood blocking as required
9. Structural steel
10. Sliding metal frame glass doors
11. Wood frame insect screens beyond
12. Wood deck steps
13. Treated wood stringer
14. Treated wood ledger
15. Treated wood joists
16. Concrete retaining wall
17. Driveway surface
18. Pile cap
19. Taper joist
20. Flashing
21. Roof membrane
22. 2 x blocking under joist to create space for conduits
23. Conduit/piping
24. Wood ceiling panels
25. Wood wall panels
26. Light fixture
27. Light cove
28. Wood flooring
29. ¾″ ply subfloor
30. Wood joists
31. Cement board
32. Wood siding
33. Building membrane wraps under roof membrane
34. Custom wood cabinets
35. Wood blocking to create slope
36. Joist to beam connection
37. Metal frame window
38. ¾″ plywood sheathing
39. Steel beam connecting to wood joists
40. Line of foundation wall beyond

Wall section at great room structural line D

Wall section at great room structural line C

The living and dining areas combine to
form a great room with a wall of sliding
doors opening the space to the deck
and pool.

149

En suite bathrooms have become a popular design choice to create spacious and bright rooms, which also are space efficient.

150

Circulation is an important aspect of en suite bathrooms. It contributes to the creation of convenient layouts that are as inviting as they are comfortable.

DIRECTORY

A Parallel Architecture
Austin, Texas, United States
www.aparallel.com

Anmahian Winton Architects
Cambridge, Massachusetts, United States
http://aw-arch.com

Antoni Associates
Cape Town, South Africa
www.aainteriors.co.za

assembleSTUDIO
Las Vegas, Nevada, United States
www.assemblagestudio.com

B.E Architecture
Prahran, Victoria, Australia
www.bearchitecture.com

Batay-Csorba Architects
Toronto, Ontario, Canada
www.batay-csorba.com

Ben Hansen Architect
New York, New york, United States
www.brharchitect.com

Blouin Tardif Architecture-Environnement
Montreal, Quebec, Canada
www.btae.ca

Brillhart Architecture
Miami, Florida, United States
http://brillhartarchitecture.com

Bruns Architecture
Milwaukee, Wisconsin, United States
http://brunsarchitecture.com

Carney Logan Burke Architects
Jackson, Wyoming, United States
www.clbarchitects.com

CAST Architecture
Seattle, Washington, United States
www.castarchitecture.com

DADA & partners
Haryana, India
http://dadapartners.com

Drew Mandel Architects
Toronto, Ontario, Canada
www.drewmandelarchitects.com

Dwell Development
Seattle, Washington, United States
http://dwelldevelopment.com

Dynia Architects
Jackson, Wyoming, United States
Denver, Colorado, United States
www.dynia.com

57STUDIO
Santiago, Chile
www.57studio.com

FINNE Architects
Seattle, Washington, United States
www.finne.com

Floriana Interiors
San Francisco, California, United States
www.florianainteriors.com

HASSELL
Adelaide, Brisbane, Melbourne, Perth, Sydney;
Australia
Beijing, Shanghai, Shenzen, Hong Kong SAR;
China
Bangkok, Thailand
Singapore, Singapore
Cardiff, London; United Kingdom
www.hassellstudio.com

Henri Cleinge, architect
Montreal, Quebec, Canada
www.cleinge.com

Hufft Projects
Kansas City, Missouri, United States
http://hufft.com

InForm
Sandringham, Brighton, Victoria, United States
www.informdesign.com.au

John Friedman Alice Kimm Architects
Los Angeles, California, United States
http://www.jfak.net

KCA
Toronto, Ontario, United States
www.kyraclarksonarchitect.ca

Lake|Flato Architects
San Antonio, Texas, United States
www.lakeflato.com

MODERNest
Toronto, Ontario, Canada
www.modernest.ca

Moloney Architects
Ballarat, Victoria, Australia
www.moloneyarchitects.com.au

NDA Natalie Dionne Architecture
Montreal, Quebec, Canada
www.ndarchgitecture.net

Ole Sondresen Architect
New York, New York, United States
www.olesondresen.com

Rangr Studio
New York, New York, United States
www.rangr.com

Robert M. Gurney, Architect
Washington, District of Columbia, United States
www.robertgurneyarchitect.com

Ruhl Walker Architects
Boston, Massachusetts, United States
http://ruhlwalker.com

SAOTA
Cape Town, Durban, South Africa
www.saota.com

Splyce Design
Vancouver, British Columbia, Canada
http://splyce.ca

Standard
Los Angeles, California, United States
www.standardarchitecture.com

Swatt Miers Architects
Emeryville, California, United States
www.swattmiers.com

The Ranch Mine
Phoenix, Arizona, United States
www.theranchmine.com